BAKE

with

Benoit Blin

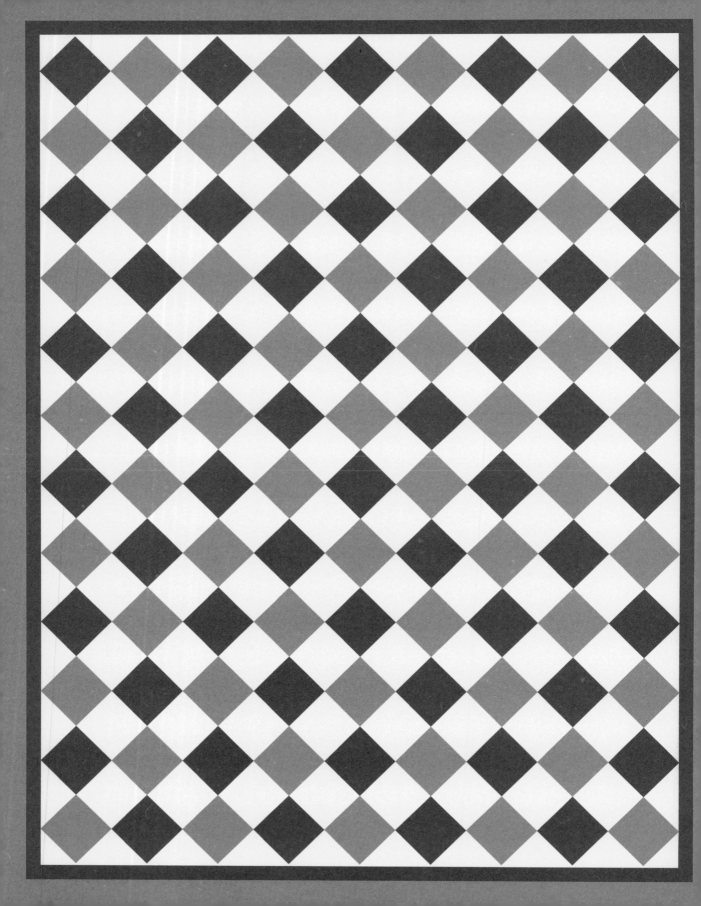

BAKE

with Benoit Blin

MASTER
CAKES, PASTRIES
and DESSERTS
LIKE A PRO

Photography by Sam Folan

Hardie Grant

B O O K S

CONTENTS

foreword by Raymond Blanc OBE
.... 6

introduction 10

BASICS

SABLÉ PASTRY TART CASE 24
SHORTCRUST PASTRY TART
  CASE 28
QUICK PUFF PASTRY 30
CHOUX PASTRY 34
CROISSANT DOUGH 39
BRIOCHE DOUGH 42
BISCUIT CUILLÈRE SPONGE 44
DACQUOISE MERINGUE 48
FRENCH CRÊPES 52
VICTORIA SPONGE 53
PASTRY CREAM 54
ALMOND CREAM 56
VANILLA CRÈME ANGLAISE 57
BUTTERCREAM 58
CHANTILLY CREAM 59
PISTACHIO PASTE 60
HOT CHOCOLATE SAUCE 60
APPLE COMPÔTE 62
LEMON BUTTERSCOTCH
  SAUCE 63
CHOCOLATE TECHNIQUES 64
EGG WASH 70
SUGAR SYRUP 70
COFFEE EXTRACT 71

SHORTBREAD & BISCUITS

CRACK-CAO BISCUITS 76
TRIPLE CHOCOLATE CHIP
  AMERICAN-STYLE COOKIES 78
VANILLA DIAMOND
  SHORTBREADS 81
BRITTANY SHORTBREADS 84
PALMIERS 86

VIENNOISERIES

CROISSANTS 90
PAIN AUX RAISINS 94
CHOCOLATE & PISTACHIO
  PAIN SWISS 96
ALMOND CROISSANTS 101
BRIOCHE LOAF 104
LITTLE BRIOCHE ROLLS 108
BRIOCHE CRÈME 107
CANDIED FRUIT BRIOCHE 112
PASSION FRUIT
  DOUGHNUTS 114
CHELSEA BUNS 116
APPLE KOUIGN-AMANN 120

PIES & TARTS

APRICOT TART BOULANGÈRE 124
MY APPLE PIE 126
RHUBARB & CUSTARD TART 130
MILLIONAIRE'S CHOCOLATE
  TART 132
GÂTEAU BASQUE 134
TARTE TATIN 138
STRAWBERRY & PISTACHIO
  TART 143
CUSTARD TART 144
PEAR ALMONDINE TART 146
FLAN VANILLE 149

TRAVEL CAKES

◆◆◆

BLUEBERRY MUFFINS	152
MUSCOVADO & DARK RUM FRUIT CAKE	154
MARBLE CAKE	156
MADELEINES	158
RASPBERRY FINANCIERS	160
SCONES	163
CHOCOLATE SCONES	164
BANANA & RUM CAKE	165
GLUTEN-FREE LEMON DRIZZLE CAKE	166
YOGHURT CAKE	168

Bon Appétit!

PETITS GATEAUX

◆

BLUEBERRY & KIRSCH TARTLETS	210
SUMMER BERRY JÉSUITES	212
MACARONS	214
POLONAISE BRIOCHE	216
COFFEE ÉCLAIRS	218
THE OPÉRA PETIT GATEAU	221

DESSERTS

SUMMER BERRY VICTORIA SPONGE	172
CRÊPES SUZETTE	174
VANILLA CRÈME CARAMEL	176
COFFEE & ORANGE CRÈME BRÛLÉE	179
WAFFLES	180
LE RIZ AU LAIT	182
CHOCOLATE FONDANT	184
HAZELNUT PARIS BREST	186
BLACKCURRANT CHARLOTTE	190
COFFEE & CARDAMOM TIRAMISU	194
CHOCOLATE & VANILLA PROFITEROLES	198
STRAWBERRY FINANCIERS	200
HOT SOUFFLÉS	204

SHOWSTOPPERS

PAVLOVA	226
CHOCOLATE CRUMBLE	230
LEMON & GRAPEFRUIT DACQUOISE	234
ORANGE SAVARIN	238
JUJU'S 'ULTRA' CHOCOLATE SPONGE CAKE	240
PINEAPPLE BAKED FLOATING ISLAND	244

index	248
thanks	254

Dear Reader,

Every Frenchman believes that his mum is the greatest cook; let me tell you a little story which illustrates this point. One day Benoit and I were chatting when he happened to mention that his mother made the best rice pudding. I was aghast. 'Non, non, non,' I said. 'That is not possible. It is *my* mum who definitely makes the best rice pudding.' Trivial to some, but to us this was deadly serious. We were both defending the honour of our mums, the regions where we grew up, and the honour of our families.

Well, soon we had gathered our ingredients, and back-to-back, fully focused, we began our task of cooking. The sweet aroma of vanilla soon filled the patisserie section of our kitchen. Then it was time to taste, and chefs and pâtissiers were the judges. Ah, that moment of tension. 'And the winner is …' Thank God, it was a draw. We had both saved the honour of our respective mums. Phew!

Many will agree when I say that Benoit is among the very best pâtissiers in Great Britain. His management skills are immense. He is the master of organisation, has a passion for excellence, and exudes an incredibly creative force. He has a gift for teaching and empowering young people, and has trained plenty of the top pâtissiers in the UK and beyond.

In *Bake with Benoit Blin*, his debut book, he is able to distil the complexity of Le Manoir's patisserie into heavenly desserts that each of you will want to cook in your own kitchen. Indeed you shall succeed and become (more of) a hero to your family and friends.

In the process of writing this book, he realised how different (and how much harder) it was to cook by himself in his own kitchen, rather than to be surrounded and supported by a brigade of twelve pâtissiers. There was a lot of sweat, though he has done all the hard work to make things far easier for you. What follows is a glorious feast of tempting dishes, from total simplicity to the more elaborate challenges, which you will still be tempted to take on. There are for example, Brittany shortbreads, divine madeleines and biscuits à la cuillère (ladyfinger sponges); you will revisit the humble Victoria sponge, and discover showstopping desserts like the pavlova or the floating island.

I must confide in you that, back in the mid-90s, it took me six months to 'woo' Benoit to work with me at Le Manoir aux Quat'Saisons. By then, he had worked for almost four years at The Ritz in Paris. Why, he argued, should he come to a country with bad weather, and some pretty terrible food? Finally, he announced that he didn't speak English. All of these were solid arguments. Still, I tried convincing him that he would have the best team around him, the best tools, that we were ambitious and that Le Manoir had two Michelin stars, with 27 acres of organic gardens providing fruit and vegetables. I also reassured him that the weather was getting better, some artisanal bakeries were opening, and that soon the humble doughnut would transform into the finest pâtissierie. Benoit has been with us since 1995 and, like me, he soon fell in love with Britain. He is now our Executive Head Pâtissier, and has received many accolades during his own career including being named Head Pastry Chef of the Year in 2009. Benoit was instrumental in showcasing the craft of pâtisserie in the UK and helped to put British pâtissiers on the world stage.

I eventually learned that Benoit's wife Sophie had some influence on his decision to come to England. Merci, Sophie.

Voilà! I will leave you to have fun as you bake with Benoit and enjoy this beautiful book. It is a wonderful testament to my friend's extraordinary skills. And I must admit, his mum's rice pudding is exceptional. Bon appétit!

Raymond Blanc OBE

CHEF PATRON, LE MANOIR AUX QUAT'SAISONS

WELCOME

My passion for baking started when I was a small boy and I fell in love with the little financier, a very rich almond sponge which I still absolutely adore. At the young age of 14, I started an apprenticeship as a baker and then a pastry chef, having spent most of my previous holidays working at the same local bakery. You could say that I fell into the sweet potion like Obelix in *The Adventures of Asterix*.

I have been Raymond Blanc's chef pâtissier at Le Manoir aux Quat'Saisons for over 25 years – running the bakery and pastry section, teaching a variety of courses at the Raymond Blanc Cookery School and helping with the creation and writing of the dessert recipes in most of Raymond's cookbooks. Throughout my early career, I trained amongst the best pastry chefs in France, and as a young man I also worked at The Ritz in Paris, where I developed the confidence and skills which allowed me to take on my position at Le Manoir in 1995, and more recently to become a judge and host on *Bake Off: The Professionals*.

Working in professional kitchens, I developed a clear understanding of what people want to eat when they come to a restaurant: they want to be surprised and excited by pastries and desserts. It was only when the lockdowns happened during the Covid pandemic that I started thinking about how people bake and eat at home, and how I'd like to teach them how to bake brilliantly in their own kitchens.

With time unexpectedly on my hands, I found myself using my skills and knowledge to bake for my family in our home kitchen. My daughter wanted a British-style ultra-rich chocolate sponge cake for her birthday; my wife suffered from nostalgia and wanted me to recreate classic French recipes, like the Gâteau Basque (which I had to adapt with prunes and raspberries), Coffee Éclairs and a Paris–Brest. As for my son, he enjoyed pretty much anything I baked and developed an interest in helping me in the kitchen. He could not get enough of the Pain aux Raisins viennoiserie, which reminded him of our travels back in France. On top of that came a few requests from schools to prepare short videos of very simple recipes for kids, such as Raspberry Financiers or a Yoghurt Cake that they could be inspired by and recreate easily at home.

I realised almost immediately that my kitchen was not actually kitted out with the equipment I take for granted when I bake in the comfort of my professional workplace. Every time I turned around, I was missing small items, such as the correct nozzle, a silicone mat, the perfect whisk. The trays were not flat enough, the oven was too small and the moulds, even if I had the right one, were of a different size or shape. Finally, difficulty in getting hold of ingredients often meant that I had to adapt or choose a recipe that I could actually bake.

As challenging as this was, I found myself enjoying the process of looking for, modifying, adapting and compiling a number of recipes to meet my family's demands. This got me thinking that with 40-years-plus experience in France and the UK as a professional pastry chef, writing a book would be an opportunity for me to share some of these recipes, with the added bonus of including professional techniques, tricks and secrets all in one place.

Encouraging, motivating and developing bakers, both in professional kitchens and at home, is really important to me. This book will demystify techniques, and make patisserie and beautiful, simple desserts or elaborate showstoppers accessible to all. You'll find simple and fresh flavours here, all inspired by my childhood in France, places I've travelled and flavours I've tried and adored, and shared as a tribute to the people I've met and loved throughout my life.

what to expect

This book is a sweet collection of cakes, bakes and desserts. Chapters are divided into type of bake:

BASICS:

Here you'll find a small selection of core recipes that enable you to make a lot of the bakes in the book, and you can even use them as a foundation to create your own recipes. Doughs, meringue, creams, pastes, sauces — this section will be your most bookmarked.

VIENNOISERIES:

These are classic viennoiseries: make a batch of the Croissant Dough on page 39 and split it between your favourite pastry recipes — Croissant, Pain aux Raisins, Almond Croissant and Pain Swiss are all included here. The same goes for the Brioche Dough on page 42 — you will find a selection of recipes to try as you perfect your brioche.

BISCUITS:

Most of these are very simple. I urge you to make a big batch — bake some straight away and then keep some in the freezer ready to bake later. Easy, simple, delicious.

TRAVEL CAKES:

Why do I call them travel cakes? These are easily transportable — they won't spill out any fillings or break while you're on the go. You'll find a lot of the easier recipes here, but they are definitely not lacking in flavour.

PIES & TARTS:

It's in the title! From a very classic French Tarte Tatin to a couple of versions of custard tarts — French and English (you decide which is best!). A fruity chapter where you can use what's in season.

DESSERTS:

Here you'll make individual servings, such as Chocolate Fondants, and sharing desserts like a Summer Berry Victoria Sponge. You'll also find classic recipes with a twist on the ingredients, such as Coffee & Orange Crème Brûlée.

PETIT GATEAUX:

This is named after the individual pastries you will find in patisseries in France. Delicate and beautiful, and layered with flavour.

SHOWSTOPPERS:

The most complex recipes in the book, because together, we can. They may sound complicated, but they are never too complex. I've shared techniques and methods that make them achievable for everybody — you just need to put a little dedication and time into the recipe.

the levels

There are three levels of difficulty in the
recipes. These are included to give you an idea
of the amount of time, difficulty of technique
and the level of organisation required to
create these bakes.

If you wanted to, you could use the book as a kind of
cookery course and start with the sweet and simple
recipes, working your way through them to bake like a
pro. I want to help you to improve your baking
confidence and skills.

◆◇◇ SWEET AND SIMPLE
◆◆◇ FOR BAKING STARS
◆◆◆ BAKE LIKE A PRO

Relatively easy recipes which everyone should be able to
achieve with minimal effort and experience, such as my
mother's Rice Pudding (for me the best in the world), a
simple Raspberry Financier, a Blueberry Muffin with a
crispy top, or a creamy Crème Caramel.

FOR BAKING STARS

Aimed at those who have spent a bit of time in the
kitchen and have more experience, these recipes require
a little more attention, skill and possibly time, but
everyone willing to have a go should be able to achieve
perfect results. There are slightly more challenging
methods, such as mastering a Croissant or Brioche
Dough, revisiting Millionaire's Shortbread and
transforming it into the most delicious sharing dessert
with a lighter texture and powerful flavours, and having
a go at building a beautiful Strawberry Pistachio Tart, a
Gâteau Basque or a Hazelnut Paris–Brest.

BAKE LIKE A PRO

Definitely for someone who is confident and feels
ready to invest a bit more time and effort in the comfort
of their own kitchen, these recipes require slightly more
work and organisation than the other levels, though
they are not complex or overly complicated. You'll
learn more professional techniques, such as tempering
chocolate and creating chocolate curls and you'll
pull together showstoppers such as Pineapple
Baked Floating Island and beautiful classic Opéra
Petit Gâteau.

Sablé Pastry Tart case (*page 24*)
Shortcrust Pastry Tart case (*page 28*)
French Crêpes (*page 52*)
Victoria Sponge (*page 53*)
Pastry Cream (*page 54*)
Almond Cream (*page 56*)
Vanilla Crème Anglaise (*page 57*)
Buttercream (*page 58*)
Chantilly Cream (*page 59*)
Pistachio Paste (*page 60*)
Hot Chocolate Sauce (*page 60*)
Apple Compôte (*page 62*)
Lemon Butterscotch sauce (*page 63*)
Egg Wash (*page 70*)
Sugar Syrup (*page 70*)
Crack-cao Biscuits (*page 76*)
Triple Choc Chip Cookies (*page 78*)
Vanilla Diamond Shortbreads (*page 81*)
Brittany Shortbreads (*page 84*)
Apricot Tarte Boulangère (*page 124*)
Apple Pie (*page 126*)
Rhubarb & Custard Tart (*page 130*)
Blueberry Muffins (*page 152*)
Muscovado and Dark Rum Fruit Cake (*page 154*)
Double Chocolate and Vanilla Marble Cake
  (*page 156*)
Madeleines (*page 158*)
Raspberry Financiers (*page 160*)
Scones (*page 163*)
Chocolate Scones (*page 164*)
Banana & Rum Cake (*page 165*)
Gluten-free Lemon Drizzle (*page 166*)
Yoghurt Cake (*page 168*)
Summer Berry Victoria Sponge (*page 172*)
Crêpes Suzette (*page 174*)
Vanilla Crème Cramel (*page 176*)
Coffee and Orange Crème Brûlée (*page 179*)
Waffles (*page 180*)
Le Riz au Lait (*page 182*)

Coffee Extract (*page 71*)
Palmiers (*page 86*)
Croissants (*page 90*)
Pain aux Raisins (*page 94*)
Chocolate Pistachio Pain Swiss (*page 96*)
Almond Croissants (*page 101*)
Brioche Loaf (*page 104*)
Little Brioche Rolls (*page 108*)
Brioche Crème (*page 109*)
Candied Fruit Brioche (*page 112*)
Passion Fruit Doughnuts (*page 114*)
Chelsea Buns (*page 116*)
Gateau Basque (*page 134*)
Tarte Tatin (*page 138*)
Strawberry Pistachio Tart (*page 143*)
Custard Tart (*page 144*)
Pear Almondine (*page 146*)
Flan Vanille (*page 149*)
Chocolate Fondant (*page 184*)
Hazelnut Paris–Brest (*page 186*)
Chocolate & Vanilla Profiteroles (*page 198*)
Strawberry Financier (*page 200*)
Blueberry and Kirsch Tartelettes (*page 210*)
Summer Berry Jésuites (*page 212*)
Macarons (*page 214*)
Coffee Éclairs (*page 218*)
Pavlova (*page 226*)

Chocolate Techniques (*page 64*)
Apple Kouign Amann (*page 120*)
Blackcurrant Charlotte (*page 190*)
Coffee and Cardamom Tiramisu (*page 194*)
Hot Soufflés (*page 204*)
Opéra Petit Gâteau (*page 221*)
Polonaise Brioche (*page 216*)
Chocolate Crumble (*page 230*)
Lemon and Grapefruit Dacquoise (*page 234*)
Orange Savarin (*page 238*)
Juju's Ultra-chocolate Sponge Cake (*page 240*)
Pineapple Baked Floating Island (*page 244*)

Quick Puff Pastry (*page 30*)
Choux Pastry (*page 34*)
Croissant Dough (*page 39*)
Brioche Dough (*page 42*)
Biscuit Cuillère Sponge (*page 44*)
Dacquoise Meringue (*page 48*)

ingredients

The recipes list all the ingredients you'll need, but here are a couple of more general notes before you get started:

Eggs are medium (55 g/2 oz on average – white 35 g/1¼ oz, yolk 20 g/¾ oz).

Butter is 80–82% fat French-style butter.

Milk is full-fat, unless stated otherwise.

Try to find the best quality you can and try to stick to the flour described in each recipe, as different flours have different percentages of protein content (i.e. gluten), and therefore different strengths. For the viennoiserie recipes, use a strong bread flour, which should contain around 12–13% protein. If you struggle to find a good one, you can also replace up to 50% of the weight of the flour with strong flour to increase the strength of the dough.

I recommend fresh yeast for most of these recipes, but if you can't find it, then you can use dried – use about half the quantity and follow the instructions on the packet.

Always use good-quality chocolate, especially when it comes to tempering, when you need a good level of cocoa butter. The price might give you an indication – generally, the more cocoa butter, the more expensive the chocolate.

equipment you may need

machinery

- Mixer with paddle, dough hook and whisk attachment
- Food processor
- *Good-quality waffle iron – traditional or electric*
- Hand blender
- *Deep-fat fryer*
- Small jug blender

pastry drawer

- Hand whisk
- Rubber spatula
- *Large palette knife*
- *Small palette knife*
- Thermometer probe
- Pastry brush
- *Piping nozzle sets (plain/fluted 6–12 cm/2½–4½ in diameter)*
- *Saint Honoré nozzle*
- Plain cutter set
- Knife set
- *Small grater (microplane)*
- Rolling pin
- *Blowtorch*
- Timer

I've put together a list of equipment for you to achieve the best results. I'm aware some of these are specific but feel free to use an alternative and adapt the recipe a little to make it work. I've included everyday equipment and more specialised kit that you might want to invest in in the future (*these are in italics*).

pots & pans

- Non-stick pan sets
- Cake/tart ring:
  - 20 cm/8 in diameter x 4 cm/1½ in deep
  - *18 cm/7 in diameter x 5–6 cm/2–2½ in deep*
  - *16 cm/6¼ in diameter x 4 cm/1½ in deep*
- Baking tray:
  - 22 cm/8½ in square x 4cm/1½ in deep
  - *24 cm/9½ in square x 4 cm/1½ in deep*
- Loaf tin (26 cm/10½ in length x 9 cm/3½ in width x 8 cm/3¼ in deep)
- *Fluted loose-bottomed pie tin (20–22 cm/8–8½ in diameter x 3.5 cm /1½ in deep)*
- Flat baking trays (38 cm/15 in length x 26 cm/10½ in wide) x 2
- *Individual non-stick brioche tins (6–7cm/2½–2¾ in diameter) x 10*
- *Non-stick savarin mould (20–22 cm/8–8½ in diameter)*
- 12-hole muffin tray with moulds (6–7 cm/2½–2¾ in diameter x 4 cm/1½ in deep)
- *Non-stick madeleine tray*
- *Deep round eared dishes (11 cm/4¼ in diameter x 3–3.5 cm/1¼–1½ in deep) x 5*
- Baking mat

pastry shelf

- Bowls
- Small jug
- *Ramekins or similar (8–9 cm/3¼–3½ in diameter x 5 cm/2 in deep)*
- *Plastic pipe 3–4 cm (1¼–1½ in) x 40 cm (16 in) long for chocolate techniques*

additional bits

- *Aluminium pudding foil tins:*
  - *7 cm/2¾ in diameter x 3 cm/1¼ in deep*
  - *6 cm/2½ in diameter x 4 cm/1 in deep*
- Quick-release spray (one-calorie) or small spray bottle for oil
- Disposable piping bags
- Baking parchment
- *Plastic acetate sheets*
- Foil
- Bain-marie (choose a pan that fits your bowl and half-fill with water. Bring to a simmer and place your bowl on top)

basics

CHAPTER 1

sablé pastry tart case

Originally a sweet pastry combined with a shortbread recipe, made specifically for the Millionaire's Chocolate Tart on page 132. It has an extra-short, buttery, crumbly, sablé texture, which works very well for any tart.

◆◇◇ ─────────────

makes 1 kg (2 lb 4 oz) pastry dough
or 3 x 20 cm (8 in) tarts

PREPARATION TIME
15 minutes

COOKING TIME
12–14 minutes

SPECIAL EQUIPMENT
Mixer with paddle attachment

─────────────── INGREDIENTS ───────────────

70 g (2½ oz/½ cup) icing (powdered) sugar

100 g (3½ oz/scant ½ cup) caster (superfine) sugar

280 g (10 oz) cold unsalted butter, diced, plus extra for greasing

2 g (½ teaspoon) vanilla extract

3 g (½ teaspoon) salt

3 egg yolks

40 g (1½ oz/⅓ cup) ground almonds

55 g (2 oz/½ cup) cornflour (cornstarch)

400 g (14 oz/3¼ cups) plain (all-purpose) flour

─────────── METHOD ───────────

MAKING THE PASTRY

1. In the mixer with the paddle attachment, combine the icing sugar, caster sugar and cold butter on a low speed. Add the vanilla extract, salt and egg yolks, and mix until incorporated.

2. Add the ground almonds, cornflour and flour, and combine for a couple of minutes until the dough comes together and looks smooth.

3. Flatten the dough until it is about 3–4 cm (1¼–1½ in) thick, then cover with cling film (plastic wrap) and leave in the refrigerator to set for at least 2 hours.

LINING & BLIND-BAKING A TART CASE

4. With your finger, spread a bit of butter around the inside of a 20 cm (8 in) tart mould or ring.

5. Roll out a disc of about 300 g (10½ oz) of the sweet pastry until 2–3 mm (1/16–⅛ in) thick. If it's a bit soft, transfer it flat onto some silicone baking parchment and return it to the refrigerator for 10–15 minutes to make it easier to handle.

6. Place the tart ring on a baking mat or some silicone baking parchment, then place the pastry into the tart ring, pushing it down gently into the base. Trim the edges, rolling over them with the rolling pin or with a knife, and place in the refrigerator to set.

7. Preheat the oven to 170°C fan (340°F).

8. Bake the tart case for 12–14 minutes, or until nice and golden. Remove from the oven, leave to cool a little, then remove the tart ring.

See step-by-step images overleaf

─────────── CHEF'S TOUCHES ───────────

You can divide the whole pastry recipe into three equal parts, *then flatten into squares, roll in cling film (plastic wrap) and keep in the freezer.*

When needed, remove from the freezer *and place in the refrigerator for 2–3 hours to defrost.*

shortcrust pastry tart case

makes 500 g (1 lb 2 oz) pastry dough or
2 x 20 cm (8 in) tarts

PREPARATION TIME
15 minutes, plus 45 minutes resting

COOKING TIME
25 minutes

SPECIAL EQUIPMENT
Mixer with paddle attachment

INGREDIENTS

250 g (9 oz/2 cups) plain (all-purpose) flour
125 g (4½ oz) cold unsalted butter, diced into 1–2 cm (½–¾ in) cubes, plus extra for greasing
40 g (1½ oz/3¼ tablespoons) caster (superfine) sugar
6 g (⅛ oz/1 teaspoon) salt
15 g (1 tablespoon) water
5 g (⅛ oz/1 teaspoon) lemon juice
1 large egg, beaten

CHEF'S TOUCHES

You can also divide the whole pastry recipe into two equal parts, *flatten into squares, roll in cling film (plastic wrap) and keep in the freezer. When needed, remove from the freezer and place in the refrigerator for 2–3 hours to defrost.*

If using cling film (plastic wrap) to blind-bake, *please make sure your cling film (plastic wrap) is PVC. If not, use baking paper.*

It does what it says 'on the tin'.

METHOD

MAKING THE PASTRY

1. In the mixer with the paddle attachment, combine the flour and the butter cubes on a low speed until a breadcrumb texture.

2. In a small bowl, dissolve the sugar and salt in the water with a whisk. Add the lemon juice and the beaten egg. Add this mixture to the flour and butter and combine on a low speed for a couple of minutes. Transfer the dough onto the work surface and, without working the dough too much, finish binding the mixture, pushing it down on the surface using the palm of your hand until smooth.

3. Transfer the dough onto a tray lined with baking parchment and flatten by hand. Cover with cling film (plastic wrap) and rest in the refrigerator for at least 45 minutes.

LINING & BLIND-BAKING A TART CASE

4. With your finger, spread a bit of butter around the inside of a 20 cm (8 in) tart mould or ring and place the tart ring on a baking mat or baking parchment.

5. Roll half the dough (or about 250 g/9 oz) into a 2.5 mm (⅟₁₆ in) thick disc. Place the pastry into the tart ring, pushing the dough down carefully so it reaches into the ring base corner. Before trimming it, create an extra lip of dough at the top of the ring, gently pinching 1 cm (½ in) of dough between your thumb and your index finger all around the top. Pass the rolling pin over the top and cut away the excess dough. Gently press downward on the fatter edge to secure the dough well in place. Using a paring knife held at an angle, trim away the edge of the tart neatly around the top of the ring for a neat finish. Rest in the refrigerator until needed.

6. Preheat the oven to 170°C fan (340°F).

7. Line the tart case with a double layer of cling film with enough excess to cover the tart twice over. Fill the lined tart to the top with dried beans or uncooked rice and fold over the excess cling film to trap the rice or beans inside.

8. Bake the tart case for about 20 minutes. Remove the rice/beans pouch from the pastry case, then bake for a further 5 minutes. Remove the blind-baked tart from the oven and set aside until needed.

quick puff pastry

This quick recipe to prepare puff pastry at home gives you fantastic and very flaky results while being completely delicious and far superior to any store-bought pastry!

makes 1.25 kg (2 lb 12 oz)

PREPARATION TIME
15 minutes, plus 1½ hours resting

SPECIAL EQUIPMENT
Mixer with paddle attachment

PLANNING AHEAD
Prepare the ice-cold water in advance by adding a few ice cubes to cold water and keeping in the refrigerator for 1 hour, then measure what you need after the ice has melted.

INGREDIENTS

500 g (1 lb 2 oz/4 cups) plain (all-purpose) flour, plus extra for dusting
500 g (1 lb 2 oz) cold unsalted butter, diced into 2 cm (¾ in) cubes
250 g (9 oz/1 cup) ice-cold water, mixed with 10 g (¼ oz) salt

METHOD

MAKING THE DOUGH

1. In the mixer with the paddle attachment, mix the flour and butter (*see Chef's Touches*) on a low speed for 10 seconds. Quickly add the salted ice-cold water (*see Chef's Touches*) and combine for about 10–15 seconds until the dough comes roughly together. You should still see lumps of butter in the pastry.

2. Remove the dough from the bowl onto a floured surface. Roll out into a rectangle measuring about 55 x 20 cm (22 x 8 in) and 1–2 cm (½–¾ in) thick.

3. Perform 2 double turns: place the dough horizontally in front of you and fold both ends of the pastry into the middle to meet, then fold in half again so that the seam is vertical to you. Repeat the process quickly. Flatten with a rolling pin until 2 cm (¾ in) thick, then wrap in cling film (plastic wrap) and refrigerate for 1 hour.

4. Remove the pastry from the refrigerator and perform a single turn by folding the top third of the pastry over the middle third and the bottom third over the top (like a letter). Refrigerate for at least 30 minutes or freeze until needed, wrapped in cling film.

5. This pastry can be prepared and frozen in advance, and it can be divided into 2–3 blocks, allowing you to defrost only what you need. When defrosting, it is better to leave the pastry in the refrigerator for 2–3 hours before use.

See step-by-step images overleaf

CHEF'S TOUCHES

It is important for the butter to be cold *so that it does not blend into the flour. Retaining whole lumps of butter through the dough helps create the flaky layering.*

The iced water *ensures that the butter remains hard and helps dissolve the salt.*

For these two steps, the dough needs a double turn

choux pastry

A classic recipe in the world of patisserie used to make éclairs, choux buns, sweet or savoury pastries and many more ... To add texture to your choux buns, you can also make a vanilla craquelin to place on top and bake with the choux bun.

makes 600 g (1 lb 5 oz) or about 28 to 30 x 10–11 cm (4 x 4¼ in) éclairs or 35–40 choux buns

See step-by-step images overleaf

PREPARATION TIME
15 minutes

COOKING TIME
30 minutes

INGREDIENTS

100 g (3½ oz) unsalted butter
100 g (3½ oz/scant ½ cup) water
100 g (3½ oz/scant ½ cup) whole milk
7 g (⅛ oz/1½ teaspoons) caster (superfine) sugar
2 g (½ teaspoon) salt
130 g (4½ oz/½ cup) plain (all-purpose) flour
4 eggs (220 g/8 oz), beaten

For the vanilla craquelin (*optional*)
90 g (3¼ oz/¾ cup) plain (all-purpose) flour
90 g (3¼ oz/generous ⅓ cup) caster (superfine) sugar
75g (2½ oz) cold unsalted butter, diced

METHOD

MAKING THE PASTRY

1. Preheat the oven to 170°C fan (340°F).
2. In a medium saucepan over a medium heat, gradually melt the butter with the water, milk, sugar and salt. Bring to a rolling boil for 30 seconds, then take the pan off the heat and, using a wooden spoon, quickly stir in the flour for about a minute until fully combined. The mixture needs to come away from the edge of the pan into a smooth dough.
3. Transfer the dough into a bowl to cool down slightly, then slowly incorporate half of the beaten eggs. Once combined, add the remaining eggs and continue to beat until the mix is a smooth and a pipeable texture. To check the texture, pick up some dough with the wooden spoon or a spatula and tilt it sideways – the dough should be trying to fall off the spatula but not quite doing it.
4. Pipe the desired sizes and shapes and bake for about 30–35 minutes (*see Chef's Touches*). Remove from the oven and leave to cool.
5. At this stage, the choux can be frozen in plastic bags, but I prefer them fresh.

MAKING THE VANILLA CRAQUELIN

6. Rub together the flour, sugar and diced cold butter to form a fine crumb. Keep working until all the ingredients come together to form a uniform dough.
7. Roll out the dough between two sheets of baking parchment until 2–3 mm (¹⁄₁₆–⅛ in) thick. Refrigerate for at least 30 minutes until needed, or freeze the craquelin dough to use later.

CHEF'S TOUCHES

As you can find different-sized eggs, *make sure you weigh your eggs for this recipe to get consistent results. You may find the result is totally different depending on how soft or firm your choux gets.*

Do not overfill your oven if your oven is small. *Bake one tray of choux at the time or there will be too much steam in the oven, which means your buns may get out of shape and collapse.*

Do not open the oven door *until the choux pastry is totally baked and has secured a firm crust or it will collapse.*

croissant dough

makes 22–24 croissants

This dough is the base for making the famous croissant at home, but not only that, I make a few other delicious pastries with it in the Viennoiseries chapter. This will make enough dough for one of those recipes, or you can split the dough between different recipes.

PREPARATION TIME
20 minutes, plus 4 hours resting

SPECIAL EQUIPMENT
Mixer with hook attachment and thermometer probe (optional)

PLANNING AHEAD
Make space in the refrigerator and allow 4 hours to make your dough. Prepare a chilled baking tray.

INGREDIENTS

220 g (8 oz) good-quality unsalted butter (82% fat)

For the dough
500 g (1 lb 2 oz/4 cups) very good-quality strong bread flour (11–13% protein content is ideal), plus extra for dusting
150 g (5½ oz/scant ⅔ cup) cold water

90 g (3¼ oz/6 tablespoons) whole milk
60 g (2 oz/¼ cup) caster (superfine) sugar
12 g (¼ oz/2½ teaspoons) salt
35 g (1¼ oz) fresh yeast
60 g (2 oz) unsalted butter, softened

INGREDIENTS

Choosing a very good bread flour *with a high protein percentage helps give a good lift to the croissants and a nice honeycomb texture.*

CHEF'S TOUCHES

For extra strength in the dough, *or if you feel your croissants are a little flat, you can use 400 g (14 oz) bread flour and 100 g (3¼ oz/generous ¾ cup) strong Canadian flour.*

See step-by-step images overleaf

METHOD

MAKING THE DOUGH

1. In the mixer with the dough hook attachment, mix all the dough ingredients on a low speed for 5 minutes, then increase the speed to medium for 10–12 minutes, or until the mixture reaches 27–28°C (81°F) maximum. Flatten the dough into a 20 cm (8 in) square, then cover with cling film (plastic wrap) and chill in the refrigerator for 2–3 hours.
2. To prepare the butter for the lamination, flatten the butter with a rolling pin into a 17 cm (6½ in) square, 1 cm (½ in) thick. Chill in the refrigerator next to the croissant dough.

SHAPING & LAMINATING THE DOUGH

3. On a floured surface, roll out the cold croissant dough into a rectangle measuring 36 x 17cm (14½ x 6½ in) and about 2 cm (¾ in) thick.
4. Position the dough horizontally and place the cold square of butter in the centre. Wrap the butter in the dough and roll out into a rectangle measuring 60 x 20 cm (24 x 8 in).
5. Position the dough lengthways and create a single turn by folding the top third of the pastry over the middle third and the bottom third over the top (like a letter). Refrigerate for at least 1 hour.
6. Remove from the refrigerator and repeat the rolling – place the seam of the pastry vertical to you. This time, the folding will need to become a double turn, by folding both ends of the pastry into the middle to meet and then folding one side over the other (like a book).
7. Roll out with a rolling pin until 2 cm (¾ in) thick, then cover with cling film and refrigerate for at least 1 hour.
8. At this stage, the dough is now ready to use to make Croissants (*see page 90*), Pain Swiss (*see page 96*), Pain aux Raisins (*see page 94*) or Almond Croissants (*see page 101*). You may choose to use half of the dough in one recipe and the other half in another.
9. When you come to rolling later on, apply gentle pressure with the rolling pin across the dough to secure it in place.

brioche dough

makes 3 large brioche (1.1 kg/2 lb 7 oz dough)

A very rich and buttery brioche dough is an absolute must in the pastry chef's recipe kit, used plain in different shapes and sizes or combined with dried fruit and pastry cream (*see pages 104, 106, 107 and 112*).

PREPARATION TIME
30 minutes, plus at least 2 hours resting

SPECIAL EQUIPMENT
Mixer with dough hook attachment

PLANNING AHEAD
Make this recipe the day before or at least 2–3 hours in advance to allow the dough to set nicely in the fridge and make it easier to work with and shape.

INGREDIENTS

500 g (1 lb 2 oz/4 cups) strong bread flour (or you could use 400 g (14 oz/3¼ cups) bread flour and 100 g (3½ oz/ generous ¾ cup) strong Canadian flour
5 eggs (55 g/2 oz each)
50 g (1¾ oz/¼ cup) caster (superfine) sugar
25 g (1 oz) fresh yeast
10 g (¼ oz) salt
45 ml (1¾ fl oz/3½ tablespoons) milk
225 g (8 oz) unsalted butter, cubed, at room temperature

CHEF'S TOUCHES

Depending on the machine speed, *you will need a low to medium setting, not too fast.*

METHOD

1. In the mixer with the hook attachment, combine all the ingredients, except the butter, on a low speed for 5 minutes. Increase the speed slightly to 2 (*see Chef's Touches*) and mix for about 12 minutes maximum, or until the dough stops sticking to the sides of the bowl. (It will start to wrap around the hook and come away from the sides of the bowl.)

2. Add the butter on a low–medium speed for 2–3 minutes until fully incorporated. Transfer the dough onto a cold tray lined with silicone baking parchment and cover it with cling film (plastic wrap). Transfer to the refrigerator to set overnight, covered, or for at least 2–3 hours.

3. Divide and shape the dough as required in the recipe, then prove and bake.

biscuit cuillère sponge

This classic finger sponge recipe is fairly simple to make and can be used across this book in different way, such as the Blackcurrant Charlotte (*see page 190*) and Coffee & Cardamom Tiramisu (*see page 194*).

makes about 2 Blackcurrant Charlottes (*see page 190*) or 2 tiramisu (*see page 194*), or a 40 x 25cm (16 x 10 in) sheet of sponge (*see Chef's Touches*)

PREPARATION TIME
15 minutes

COOKING TIME
10 minutes

SPECIAL EQUIPMENT
Mixer with whisk attachment, piping bag and plain 1 cm (½ in) nozzle, electric whisk, 40 x 25cm (16 x 10 in) flat baking tray

INGREDIENTS

4 eggs, yolks and whites separated (approx. 140g (5 oz) whites and 80 g (2¾ oz) yolks)
80 g (2¾ oz/⅓ cup) caster (superfine) sugar
80 g (2¾ oz/⅔ cup) plain (all-purpose) flour, sifted

CHEF'S TOUCHES

You can also bake a sheet of sponge using this recipe *to make a nice Swiss roll, or cut out discs to make desserts like the tiramisu, but this may create a little bit more wastage.*

When you first mix your egg whites and egg yolks, they do not have to be fully combined, *as you will continue to mix them when you add the flour. If you over fold the mixture, it will collapse. This technique helps you to retain as much volume and lightness as possible.*

The tiramisu disc will be used inside an 18 cm (7 in) ring, *but it needs to be slightly smaller than the ring itself so that it won't show on the dessert later, so slightly mark this inside the ring on the paper or trim the sponge once baked.*

To check if your sponge is baked, *gently press the top of the sponge with the tip of your finger — it should spring back up straight away.*

METHOD

PREPARING THE SPONGE MIXTURE

1. Put the egg whites into the bowl of a stand mixer with a whisk attachment and the egg yolks into a medium bowl. Add half the sugar to the egg whites and beat on full speed until soft peaks form, then gradually add the remaining sugar. Continue until firm with stiff peaks.

2. With a hand whisk, add a quarter of the whipped egg white to the bowl of egg yolks and, gently mix. Using a rubber spatula, lightly fold this mixture back lightly into the remaining egg white (*see Chef's Touches*). Add the flour and combine for a few seconds only, without collapsing the mixture.

PREPARING THE SPONGE DISC FOR TIRAMISU

3. Preheat the oven to 190°C fan (400°F).

4. Using a plain 1 cm (½ in) nozzle, pipe 17 cm (6½ in) discs, 1 cm (½ in) deep over a flat tray lined with baking parchment (*see Chef's Touches*). This recipe will give you more than enough mixture. You will only need two discs for the tiramisu on page 194, so you can pipe more and keep them in the freezer.

PIPING THE SPONGE FOR BLACKCURRANT CHARLOTTE

5. Please see the piping method in the Blackcurrant Charlotte recipe on page 190 and images overleaf, then dust with the icing sugar before baking.

BAKING THE SPONGE SHEET OR DISCS

6. Preheat the oven to 190°C fan (375°F). Line a 40 x 25cm (16 x 10 in) baking tray with a sheet of baking parchment. Spread the sponge mixture over the top and level nicely with a palette knife.

7. Bake in the middle of the oven for 8–10 minutes until light blond with a spongy texture (*see Chef's Touches*). Leave on the side to cool for 10 minutes, then slide the sponge out of the tray onto a cooling rack. When needed, flip the sheet of sponge upside down and carefully peel off the baking parchment. Use as instructed in your recipe.

See step-by-step images overleaf

Piping the Blackcurrant Charlotte (page 190)

dacquoise
meringue

makes a 20 cm (8 in) dacquoise (*see Chef's Touches*)

PREPARATION TIME
10–15 minutes

COOKING TIME
25 minutes

SPECIAL EQUIPMENT
Hand whisk, hand-held electric whisk or small mixer with whisk attachment, piping bag with a large plain nozzle (12 mm/½ in diameter), 20 cm (8 in) cake ring, approx. 4.5 cm (1¾ in) deep

INGREDIENTS

75 g (2½ oz/¾ cup) ground almonds
60 g (2 oz/½ cup) icing (powdered) sugar
15 g (½ oz/1 tablespoon) cornflour (cornstarch)
70 g (2½ oz) fresh egg whites
60 g (2 oz/¼ cup) caster (superfine) sugar

The recipe is called a dacquoise because it is believed to have been created in the city of Dax in the south of France. It is an almond or hazelnut meringue, crispy on the outside and slightly soft in the middle, which gives a rich texture to any dessert.

METHOD

1. Preheat the oven to 170°C fan (340°F). Line a flat baking tray with baking parchment and line the inside of the cake ring with a band of baking parchment the same height as the ring.

2. In a medium bowl, whisk together the ground almonds, icing sugar and cornflour. In the mixer with the whisk attachment, whip the egg whites on a high speed until medium peaks form. Gradually add the sugar and continue to whisk until firm peaks form. Using a rubber spatula, carefully fold in the dry ingredients for a few seconds until incorporated, trying to retain a pipeable and light texture.

3. Transfer the meringue to the piping bag with the plain nozzle and pipe large tear-shaped drops against the inside of the cake ring, towards the centre, to make it look like a large daisy. The petals should be taller than the centre.

4. Bake for about 25 minutes until nice and dry. When baked, remove from the oven, take off the cake ring and set the meringue aside to cool.

See step-by-step images overleaf

CHEF'S TOUCHES

You may want to double up the recipe, *using a stand mixer if your whisk struggles to pick up this quantity of egg whites.*

french crêpes

makes 18 crêpes

The real thin French pancake recipe. Many garnishes work so well with crêpes: simple caster sugar, or a bit of jam, or chocolate and nut spreads are just a few of the endless possibilities. To make them grand restaurant-style, turn them into Crêpes Suzette (*see page 174*) or serve them flambé with alcohol.

PREPARATION TIME
15 minutes

COOKING TIME
20 minutes

SPECIAL EQUIPMENT
Good non-stick frying pan (20 cm/8 in diameter)

PLANNING AHEAD
Make the crêpe batter 1 hour in advance.

INGREDIENTS

100 g (3½ oz) unsalted
butter, for frying

For the batter
50 g (1¾ oz) unsalted butter
200 g (7 oz/1⅔ cups)
plain (all-purpose) flour
40 g (1½ oz/3¼
tablespoons) caster
(superfine) sugar

small pinch of salt
2 medium eggs
500 ml (17 fl oz/generous
2 cups) whole milk
15 ml (1 tablespoon)
dark rum

METHOD

MAKING THE BATTER
1. Heat the butter for the batter in a frying pan over a medium heat until it foams and has a delicate nutty colour, then transfer to a small bowl and set aside to cool.
2. In a mixing bowl, combine the flour, sugar and salt. Create a well in the centre of the flour and whisk in the eggs, slowly incorporating the flour from the sides of the bowl until you have a consistent mixture. Whisk in the milk, followed by the brown butter and the rum.

COOKING THE CRÊPES
3. Heat the non-stick frying pan over a high heat until it is hot, then reduce to a medium heat and quickly melt in a small knob of butter, rotating it around the pan. Pour in a small ladle of batter and rotate the batter evenly so that it covers the whole frying pan surface. Cook for 30–40 seconds, then turn over with a spatula and cook the other side for another 30 seconds. Repeat with the remaining butter and batter.
4. Eat warm with a bit of caster sugar or pile up the crêpes on a flat, round plate as you are making them and eat them all later.

CHEF'S TOUCHES

Be careful not to overcook the butter *and turn the wonderful golden nutty butter to dark brown and black, it will then taste bitter and will not be good for you to consume.*

When cooking the pancakes, *the temperature of the pan is very important. If it is not hot enough, the pancakes will be leathery and lack colour and flavour.*

victoria sponge

This is just the sponge recipe. See page 172 for my Summer Berry Victoria Sponge.

See page 172 for my Summer Berry Victoria Sponge.

◆◇◇

makes 1 cake to serve 6–8

PREPARATION TIME
10 minutes

COOKING TIME
18–20 minutes

SPECIAL EQUIPMENT
20 cm (8 in) fluted loose-bottomed cake tin (or a plain one will do), hand whisk

PLANNING AHEAD
Take the butter out of the refrigerator and leave at room temperature to soften slightly.

INGREDIENTS

130 g (4½ oz) unsalted butter, softened, plus 20 g (¾ oz), plus 20 g (¾ oz) for greasing

130 g (4½ oz/½ cup) caster (superfine) sugar

2 eggs, beaten

80 g (2¾ oz/⅔ cup) self-raising flour (or 80 g/2¾ oz/⅔ cup plain/all-purpose flour + ½ teaspoon baking powder)

2 tablespoons ground almonds

METHOD

1. Preheat the oven to 170°C fan (340°F). Lightly brush the cake tin with the 20 g (¾ oz) softened butter and place in the refrigerator.
2. In a large bowl, whisk together the 130 g (4½ oz) soft butter and the sugar for a couple of minutes, or until light and pale in colour. Add the beaten eggs and combine until smooth. Gradually whisk in the flour and ground almonds. Using a rubber spatula, pour the sponge batter into the prepared tin and spread it evenly. Bake for 18–20 minutes (*see Chef's Touches*), or until the blade of a small paring knife comes out clean when pricked into the cake.
3. Leave to cool a little, then tip over to de-mould the sponge onto a cooling rack.

CHEF'S TOUCHES

If using a loose-bottomed cake tin, *it is always better to bake it in the middle of the oven to help the base of the cake bake evenly.*

pastry cream

The cream filling that all pastry shops and bakeries use in France. It is used to fill éclairs and choux pastry, as well as bakery items such as pain aux raisins, flans and many more. It can also be used as a base for soufflé mixtures.

makes 550 g (1 lb 4 oz)

PREPARATION TIME
5 minutes

COOKING TIME
10 minutes

SPECIAL EQUIPMENT
Small hand whisk, rubber spatula

PLANNING AHEAD
Line a cold baking tray with cling film (plastic wrap) to cool the cream in after it has been cooked.

INGREDIENTS

400 g (14 oz/generous 1½ cups) whole milk
½ vanilla pod
60 g (2 oz/¼ cup) caster (superfine) sugar
4 egg yolks
40 g (1½ oz/⅓ cup) cornflour (cornstarch)

METHOD

1. Pour the milk into a medium saucepan. Split the vanilla bean through the middle with a paring knife and scrape the seeds into the milk. Add the pod to the pan, too, then bring to the boil, whisking in a quarter of the sugar to prevent the milk from catching on the bottom of the pan.

2. Meanwhile, in a bowl, whisk together the egg yolks, cornflour and the remaining sugar. As soon as the vanilla milk boils, take it off the heat and pour a quarter of it over the yolk mixture, whisking rapidly. Still off the heat, transfer this mixture back into the pan with the remaining vanilla milk, whisking continuously. Place back over a medium heat and continue whisking until the mixture starts thickening, then and take off the heat again and continue to whisk until smooth.

3. When thickened and smooth, return the pan to the heat and bring the mixture back to the boil. Cook for 1 minute, then take the pan off the hob and remove the vanilla bean. Using a rubber spatula, transfer the cream into the cold tray lined with cling film (plastic wrap) to cool quickly. Wrap and cover the cream in the film. Set aside to cool.

4. When the cream is cold, whisk until smooth, then transfer to a covered container and reserve in the refrigerator until needed. The cream can be made up to 2–3 days in advance.

almond cream

A rich almond filling that we use as a base for tarts before baking. It brings texture and a lot of flavour to your bakes.

◆ ◆ ◆ ───────────

makes about 420 g (15 oz)

PREPARATION TIME
10 minutes

SPECIAL EQUIPMENT
Mixer with paddle attachment

PLANNING AHEAD
You can make more than you actually need and keep the rest in the freezer to use in another recipe.

1. In the mixer with the paddle attachment, cream together the butter, icing sugar and vanilla extract until slightly pale in colour. Add the ground almonds and flour and combine for 1 minute until smooth. Slowly add the beaten eggs and lastly the rum.
2. Set in an airtight container in the refrigerator until needed, it will keep for 4–5 days.

INGREDIENTS

100 g (3½ oz) unsalted butter, at room temperature

100 g (3½ oz/generous ¾ cup) icing (powdered) sugar

½ teaspoon vanilla extract

100 g (3½ oz/1 cup) ground almonds

20 g (¾ oz/2½ tablespoons) plain (all-purpose) flour (or cornflour/cornstarch if you want it to be gluten-free), sifted

2 eggs, beaten

15 ml (1 tablespoon) dark rum

CHEF'S TOUCHES

This recipe may make more than you need. *Freeze the rest in an airtight container or even in a disposable piping bag, ready to use once defrosted.*

vanilla crème anglaise

Inspired by the English custard, believe it or not, this very French vanilla sauce recipe is also a base for many desserts and ice cream.

◆◆◆

makes 600 g (1 lb 5 oz)

PREPARATION TIME
5 minutes

COOKING TIME
5 minutes

SPECIAL EQUIPMENT
Rubber spatula, thermometer probe if you have one

PLANNING AHEAD
Prepare the ice bain-marie below (*see Chef's Touches before you start*)

INGREDIENTS

6 egg yolks
65 g (2¼ oz/¼ cup) caster (superfine) sugar
500 ml (17 fl oz/generous 2 cups) whole milk
2 vanilla pods, split lengthways and scraped

METHOD

1. Place a clean medium bowl over the ice bain-marie and place it nearby, ready for when you need it later.
2. In a large mixing bowl, whisk together the egg yolks and sugar until they turn a pale straw colour.
3. Pour the milk into a medium saucepan, then add the split and scraped vanilla beans and bring to the boil. Gradually pour the hot milk over the creamed eggs and sugar, whisking continuously. Transfer the mixture back into the saucepan and cook over a medium heat to bind the custard, stirring continuously with a rubber spatula until it reaches 83–84°C (181–183°F) and has lightly thickened enough to coat the back of the spatula.
4. Take the pan off the heat and wait for about 30 seconds to allow the custard to thicken, then immediately pass the sauce through the sieve and into the bowl placed over the ice bain-marie. Continue stirring with the spatula for a few minutes to stop the sauce from cooking, and then leave to cool completely. Reserve, covered, in the refrigerator until needed. This will keep for 3–4 days.

CHEF'S TOUCHES

For the ice bain-marie, *use cold water and ice cubes in a 50:50 ratio.*

If the sauce looks a little split, *quickly whisk it for a few seconds and it should come back together.*

buttercream

makes about 380 g (13 oz)

A cooked buttercream recipe that you can use straight away or keep in the refrigerator for few days – you just need to bring it back to room temperature and whisk it to get back its creamy texture.

PREPARATION TIME
10 minutes

COOKING TIME
5 minutes

SPECIAL EQUIPMENT
Mixer with whisk attachment, temperature probe

PLANNING AHEAD
Remove the butter from the refrigerator and cut into cubes, then leave to soften 1 hour before baking.

INGREDIENTS

3 egg yolks
30 g (1 oz/2 tablespoons) cold water
100 g (3 ½ oz/scant ½ cup) caster (superfine) sugar
225 g (8 oz) unsalted butter, cubed and left at room
  temperature

METHOD

1. In a mixer, whisk the egg yolks on a medium speed until light and aerated, then continue whisking on a low speed.

2. Meanwhile, pour the cold water into a small pan, then add the sugar and cook it over a medium heat until it reaches 118°C (244°F). Lower the speed of the mixer to minimum, and quickly pour the sugar syrup over the whipped egg yolks. Bring the mixer back up to full speed straight away (*see Chef's Touches*) and continue whisking until lukewarm. At this stage, reduce the speed of the mixer to medium and gradually add the soft butter cubes. Bring the mixer back up to full speed again and continue whisking until the butter is fully combined and the cream looks smooth and
fluffy in texture. Add any flavourings you are using (*see Chef's Touches*). This will keep for 2–3 days in an airtight container stored in the refrigerator.

CHEF'S TOUCHES

At this stage, *you may need to gently lift the bowl of the mixer for a few seconds to ensure that the whisk catches as much of the cooked sugar syrup as possible and that it is fully combined with the egg yolks without any lumps.*

You can flavour your buttercream as you wish, *using coffee or vanilla extract, citrus zest like lemon, or even liqueurs like Grand Marnier or Cointreau.*

chantilly cream

This classic sweet French whipped cream recipe is the perfect companion to many desserts.

◆◇◇ ─────────────

makes about 400 g (14 oz)

PREPARATION TIME
5 minutes

SPECIAL EQUIPMENT
Hand whisk or mixer with a whisk attachment

─────────── INGREDIENTS ───────────

400 g (14 oz/1¾) whipping cream (35–40% fat)
40 g (1½ oz/⅓ cup) icing (powdered) sugar
1 teaspoon vanilla extract (*optional*)

─────────── METHOD ───────────

1. In a medium bowl or a mixer with a whisk attachment, whisk together all the ingredients until you have medium to firm peaks, or a nice creamy texture. Use straight away or reserve in the refrigerator for no more than 30 minutes–1 hour.

─────────── CHEF'S TOUCHES ───────────

You can also use a siphon gun to get a firm and fluffy texture, *for which I would recommend using 35% fat UHT whipping cream, which tends to give a lighter cream.*

pistachio paste

A good pistachio paste can be hard to find, so why not try to make your own?

◆◇◇ ─────────

makes 250 g (9 oz)

PREPARATION TIME
10 minutes

COOKING TIME
8 minutes

SPECIAL EQUIPMENT
Good small jug blender or small spice grinder

INGREDIENTS

200 g (7 oz/1⅓ cups) whole shelled green pistachios
15 g (1 tablespoon) kirsch eau de vie
40 g (1½ oz/3¼ tablespoons) caster (superfine) sugar
3 drops of almond extract (if you like a little almondy flavour in your paste)

METHOD

1. Preheat the oven to 145°C fan (290°F).
2. In a small bowl, using a spoon, coat the shelled pistachios with the kirsch eau de vie, then roll them in the sugar to coat each nut. Transfer them onto a clean baking tray and bake for about 8 minutes. Remove from the oven and leave the toasted nuts to cool completely.
3. When cool, add the nuts to the jug blender along with the almond paste (if using). Crush and blend them on full speed for about 3–4 minutes until you have a smooth paste.
4. Reserve the paste until needed. The paste should keep easily for a couple of weeks in the refrigerator, stored in an airtight container.

CHEF'S TOUCHES

Depending on the size of your food processor, *you may need to double the recipe to be able to crush the nuts quickly into a paste. Add half a tablespoon of groundnut oil to help loosen it.*

hot chocolate sauce

A moreish chocolate sauce ideal to pour over your Profiteroles (*see page 198*) or Waffles (*see page 180*).

◆◇◇ ─────────

makes 340 g (11½ oz)

PREPARATION TIME
5 minutes

INGREDIENTS

170 g (6 oz) good-quality dark chocolate (65–70% cocoa)
200 g (7 oz/scant 1 cup) whole milk

METHOD

1. Chop the chocolate into small pieces and place in a medium bowl. In a saucepan, bring the milk to the boil, then pour it over the chocolate and leave to sit for a few seconds to melt it. Whisk to combine. Use the sauce while still warm or transfer it to the refrigerator (*see Chef's Touches*).

CHEF'S TOUCHES

You can make the sauce in advance and keep it in the refrigerator for a couple of days. *You will need to warm it up for a few seconds in the microwave or using a bain-marie.*

apple compôte

◆ ◇ ◇ ─────────

makes about 600 g (1 lb 5 oz)

PREPARATION TIME
10 minutes

COOKING TIME
5–10 minutes

INGREDIENTS

170 g (6 oz) Granny Smith apple (about 1 large)

170 g (6 oz) Braeburn apples (about 1–2)

340 g (11½ oz) Bramley apples (about 2–3, depending on the size of the apples)

80 g (2¾ oz/⅓ cup) caster (superfine) sugar

8 g (¼ oz/2½ teaspoons) lemon juice

50 g (2¾ oz/3½ tablespooons) apple juice or water

I like to combine different apples when I can to get the ideal texture and flavour. You can eat this on its own or to bake it into a dessert or a tart.

METHOD

1. Peel and core the apples. Chop into 2 cm (¾ in) chunks. Add the apple chunks and remaining ingredients to a medium pan, then cover with a lid and bring to a gentle simmer over a medium heat. Cook for about 5 minutes (until the Bramley apples are broken down).

2. Remove from the heat and leave to cool to lukewarm, keeping the pan covered; the compôte will finish cooking in the residual heat. Whisk the compôte to crush it down and set aside to cool completely.

3. Cover and reserve in the refrigerator until needed. Stored in an airtight container, the compôte will keep its flavour for 2–3 days.

lemon butterscotch sauce

◆◇◇ ────────

makes 400 g (14 oz)

PREPARATION TIME
5 minutes

COOKING TIME
5 minutes

PLANNING AHEAD
Prepare a clean, shallow baking tray or a large container to cool the sauce quickly.

INGREDIENTS

75 g (2½ oz) freshly squeezed lemon juice
zest of ½ lemon (5 g/⅛ oz)
180 g (6 oz/¾ cup) whipping cream
25 g (1 oz/5 teaspoons) water

150 g (5½ oz/⅔ cup) caster (superfine) sugar
75 g (2½ oz/5 tablespoons) glucose syrup (if unavailable, replace with 50 g/1¾ oz/¼ cup caster/superfine sugar)

This little sauce works so well with chocolate, but also drizzled over an ice cream or served with a lemon tart or a lemon dessert for the perfect combination of flavours.

METHOD

1. In a small saucepan or in a bowl in the microwave, heat the lemon juice and zest. In a separate small pan, heat the whipping cream over a medium heat, bringing the cream to a simmer.
2. Meanwhile, in a high-sided medium pan set over a medium heat, dissolve the sugar and glucose in the water and then, without stirring, bring to a golden-blond caramel colour. Carefully and gradually pour the hot lemon juice on top (*see Chef's Touches*), followed gradually by the hot whipping cream. Stir well with a whisk and bring back to the boil for 1 minute.
3. Pass the sauce through a sieve and into a shallow tray to cool down quickly or alternatively into a bowl on an ice bain-marie. Stored in an airtight container in the refrigerator, the sauce will keep for 4–5 days.

CHEF'S TOUCHES

Pouring liquid over hot caramel makes it bubble up and explode a little. *If you use a high-sided saucepan to cook the caramel and you gradually pour in the lemon juice and the cream when hot, it will minimise this effect.*

Adding a little grated ginger to the cream *will also bring a bit of heat to the sauce.*

chocolate techniques

Here are three simple chocolate techniques that will be used in this book. These are not conventional, but the key is to avoid heating the chocolate to too high a temperature.

◆◆◆

PREPARATION TIME
15 minutes

SPECIAL EQUIPMENT
Simmering hot bain-marie, temperature probe, small 3 cm (1¼ in) plastic pipe or rolling pin, 2 sheets of plastic acetate or baking paper, 3 cm (1¼ in) plain cutter, 16 cm (6¼ in) cake ring

PLANNING AHEAD
Have your simmering bain-marie ready. You can prepare the chocolate work 2–3 days in advance, ready to be used in the relevant recipe

| INGREDIENTS |

150 g (5½ oz) good-quality dark or milk chocolate, chopped

| CHEF'S TOUCHES |

Without going into too much detail, *we are trying not to de-crystallise the chocolate, so we need to melt it gradually until it reaches the required temperature. Overheating the chocolate will cause it to lose its texture and smooth colour when it sets.*

When tempered correctly, *the chocolate will clone the texture of the material it has been set on; if using baking parchment, it will be dull and have a paper-like feel, but if using plastic acetate, it will be smooth and shiny.*

| METHOD |

QUICK TEMPERING METHOD

1. Using a bain-marie, gradually melt the milk chocolate to 30°C (86°F) or the dark chocolate to 31–32°C (88–90°F) maximum. Do this by dipping the bowl of chocolate into the bain-marie for 30 seconds at a time, stirring between dips.

| METHOD |

FOR CHOCOLATE CURLS

1. Temper your chosen chocolate as in the quick tempering method.
2. Prepare two sheets of baking parchment, each about 40 x 30 cm (16 x 12 in). Place one sheet on a flat table, then pour the chocolate over it in a line, 3 cm (1¼ in) from the top and the sides. Place the other sheet of parchment exactly on top and spread the melted chocolate evenly by sliding a PVC pipe or rolling pin across the paper, until you have a thin layer of chocolate (*see Chef's Touches*). Before it sets, peel the parchment sheets away from one another so you have two thin sheets of chocolate, with a similar amount on each side. Leave the chocolate to set slightly and then, with a palette knife, score diagonally in a criss-cross pattern with lines of about 6 cm (2½ in) apart. Stack the scored sheets of chocolate on top of each other and place another sheet of parchment on top. Immediately wrap the sheets around a small PVC pipe or rolling pin before the chocolate sets completely, without applying too much pressure. Place the rolled chocolate in the refrigerator to set for 1 hour minimum or until needed.
3. Remove from the refrigerator, remove the pipe or rolling pin and carefully unwrap the paper, revealing the large chocolate curls. Place the delicate curls on a flat tray or in a covered container in the refrigerator until needed.

FOR CHOCOLATE COINS & DISCS

1. For the small pennies in the Chocolate Crumble on page 230, use milk chocolate; for the chocolate disc in the Tiramisu on page 194, use dark chocolate.
2. Temper the chocolate as above, then spread it between two sheets of baking parchment or plastic acetate (*see Chef's Touches*). Allow the chocolate to partially set for a few minutes. Mark with the 3 cm (1¼ in) cutter for the pennies or the 16 cm (6¼ in) cake ring for the discs.
3. Leave to set completely between two flat trays in the refrigerator for 30 minutes, and reserve in a cool place until needed.

See step-by-step images on the following four pages

for chocolate curls

for chocolate coins

for chocolate discs

egg wash

This basic recipe is used to give a beautiful shiny glaze to all your baked viennoiseries. It can be made in advance and kept in the refrigerator, covered, or in a jar, for a couple of days.

◆◇◇ ──────

makes 140–150 g (5–5½ oz)

PREPARATION TIME
5 minutes

SPECIAL EQUIPMENT
Hand whisk

─────(INGREDIENTS)─────

2 eggs
1 egg yolk
1 teaspoon whipping cream

─────(METHOD)─────

1. In a small bowl, whisk together all the ingredients until smooth. Pass through a sieve.
2. Reserve in the refrigerator for a couple of days maximum, keeping covered until needed.

sugar syrup

This basic recipe is used a lot around a pastry kitchen, and can be kept at the back of your refrigerator in a sealed jar ready for when you need some.

◆◇◇ ──────

makes 360 g (12½ oz)

PREPARATION TIME
5 minutes

─────(INGREDIENTS)─────

200 ml (7 fl oz/scant 1 cup) water
200 g (7 oz/generous ¾ cup) caster (superfine) sugar

─────(METHOD)─────

1. Combine the sugar and water in a small saucepan and bring to the boil for 1 minute.
2. Leave to cool completely, then keep in a sealed jar or similar at the back of your refrigerator until needed – it will keep for up to two weeks.

coffee extract

makes about 200 g (7 oz)

You can buy a very good coffee extract off the shelf in shops, but in case you want to make your own, here is a simple recipe.

PREPARATION TIME
10 minutes

COOKING TIME
10 minutes

SPECIAL EQUIPMENT
Temperature probe

PLANNING AHEAD
Prepare a batch of nice strong coffee.

1. In a small/medium saucepan, combine the cold water, glucose and sugar. Bring to the boil and continue cooking until the mixture reaches 150°C (290°F) then take off the heat. Meanwhile, dissolve the instant coffee. Pour the coffee mixture over the sugar mixture in the pan, whisking it in gradually and safely (*see Chef's Touches*). When fully incorporated, transfer the mixture into a bigger pan and bring it back to the boil, then simmer over a low–medium heat for 1 minute (*see Chef's Touches*).
2. Once cool, transfer into a bottle until needed. It will keep in the cupboard for a few weeks.

INGREDIENTS

50 g (1¾ oz/3½ tablespoons) cold water
40 g (1½ oz/scant 3 tablespoons) glucose syrup
100 g (3½ oz/scant ½ cup) caster (superfine) sugar
20 g (¾ oz) good-quality instant coffee
150 g (5½ oz/scant ⅔ cup) strong hot coffee

CHEF'S TOUCHES

Ensure the coffee is very hot *and pour it slowly over the cooked sugar, as there will be a thermic shock to begin with, which can create a sudden explosion and splash out.*

The coffee extract has a tendency to suddenly boil up quickly and foam over the pan, *which is why you have to control the heat and transfer it into a bigger pan. Stay with it as you may need to take the pan off the heat. Nobody wants to clean the hob when coffee extract has boiled over!*

shortbread & biscuits

CHAPTER 2

crack-cao biscuits

makes 80 little sablés
(*see Chef's Touches*)

PREPARATION TIME
10 minutes, plus 2 hours resting

COOKING TIME
10 minutes

SPECIAL EQUIPMENT
Mixer with paddle attachment, baking mat

PLANNING AHEAD
Take the butter out of the refrigerator 2 hours before needed.

INGREDIENTS

225 g (8 oz) unsalted butter, at room temperature

300 g (10½ oz/scant 2½ cups) icing (powdered) sugar

1 egg, beaten

220 g (8 oz/1¾ cups) plain (all-purpose) flour

pinch of salt

45 g (1½ oz/⅓ cup) cocoa powder

¼ teaspoon ground cinnamon

220 g (8 oz/1¾ cups) pecan nut halves, roughly chopped

110 g (3¾ oz/¾ cup) shelled pistachios, roughly chopped

One of my favourite types of little biscuits – crispy, buttery, snappy, nutty, naughty!

METHOD

PREPARE THE DOUGH

1. In the mixer with the paddle attachment, combine the butter and icing sugar on a low speed. Gradually add the beaten egg. Sift together the flour, salt, cocoa powder and cinnamon, then add this to the butter and sugar mixture. Finally, add the chopped nuts and combine gently so as not to overwork the dough.

2. Stretch 30 cm (12 in) of cling film (plastic wrap) across the table and place one-third of the mixture at the bottom. Using the cling film, tightly roll the mixture into a 4 cm (1½ in) diameter sausage, twisting the cling film at both ends to tighten into a nice cylinder. Repeat with the remaining dough and rest in the freezer to set for at least 2 hours.

BAKING

3. Preheat the oven to 170°C fan (340°F).

4. Take a frozen cylinder of biscuit dough out of the freezer and let it come up to room temperature for 5 minutes. Using a sharp knife, slice the dough while still firm into 2–3 mm (1/16–1/8 in) thick discs and lay them flat, at least 2 cm (¾ in) apart on a baking tray lined with a baking mat. Repeat with the remaining biscuit cylinders, depending on how many biscuits you want to make.

5. Bake for about 10 minutes, rotating the tray after 5 minutes (*see Chef's Touches*). Leave to cool completely and enjoy! These are best eaten on the day, but stored in an airtight container will keep for up to 3 days.

CHEF'S TOUCHES

As it is hard to know *when the biscuits are baked due to the colour of the dough, a good way to find out is to look at the nuts, which should start to go a nice golden colour.*

You can make this dough, *freeze it in cylinders and take one out at a time to bake fresh biscuits as and when you want them!*

triple chocolate chip american-style cookies

makes 24 cookies

PREPARATION TIME
10 minutes

COOKING TIME
12 minutes

SPECIAL EQUIPMENT
Mixer with paddle attachment

Thank you to my sous chef Glen for this recipe. The whole team has enjoyed these cookies over the years.

INGREDIENTS

230 g (8 oz) unsalted butter

180 g (6 oz/¾ cup) caster (superfine) sugar

230 g (8 oz/1¼ cups) soft dark brown sugar

1 large egg, beaten

190 g (6¾ oz/1½ cups) strong flour

190 g (6¾ oz/1½ cups) plain (all-purpose) flour, plus extra for dusting

12 g (¼ oz/1 heaped tablespoon) baking powder

2 pinches of salt

200 g (7 oz) dark chocolate, chopped into small pieces

100 g (3½ oz) white chocolate, chopped into small pieces

100 g (3½ oz) milk chocolate, chopped into small pieces

CHEF'S TOUCHES

Do not overwork the dough, *as the cookies will spread out more and become flat.*

METHOD

1. Preheat the oven to 170°C fan (340°F).

2. In the mixer with the paddle attachment, combine the butter with both sugars on a medium speed for 2–3 minutes, or until it becomes pale and creamy. Add the salt and beaten egg. Sift together the flours and baking powder, then add to the butter mixture with the mixer running on a low speed. Let it combine fully for 1–2 minutes (*see Chef's Touches*).

3. Trying to mix the dough as little as possible, add the chopped chocolate pieces on a low speed and stop as soon as they have evenly spread throughout the dough. On a lightly floured surface, roll the dough into a 4 cm (1½ in) diameter cylinder and, using a serrated knife or a large kitchen knife, divide the log into 24 equal slices.

4. Place each slice flat on its side, onto a baking tray lined with baking parchment, spacing them 3 cm (1¼ in) apart. Bake for about 14 minutes until golden. Remove from the oven and leave to cool for a few minutes before eating. These are best eaten on the day, but stored in an airtight container will keep for up to 3 days.

vanilla diamond shortbreads

These little French shortbreads are rolled in granulated sugar, which makes them glitter like diamonds.

makes 30–40 small shortbreads

PREPARATION TIME
15 minutes, plus 1–1½ hours setting

COOKING TIME
8–10 minutes

SPECIAL EQUIPMENT
Mixer with paddle attachment, pastry brush

PLANNING AHEAD
Take the butter out of the refrigerator 1 hour before starting.

INGREDIENTS

150 g (5½ oz) unsalted
  butter, at room
  temperature
80g (2¾ oz/⅔ cup) icing
  (powdered) sugar
1 egg yolk
2 g (½ teaspoon) vanilla
  extract

200 g (7 oz/1⅔ cups) plain
  (all-purpose) flour
pinch of salt

To decorate
100 g (3½ oz/scant ½ cup)
  granulated sugar
1 egg, beaten

METHOD

1. In a stand mixer with the paddle attachment, combine the butter and icing sugar on a low speed. Add the egg yolk and vanilla extract, then add the flour and salt. Allow to combine for a couple of minutes, or until smooth.

2. Divide the dough equally into two pieces. Roll each piece into a 35 cm (14 in) long, 2.5 cm (1 in) diameter log and place in the refrigerator to rest and set for 45 minutes–1 hour (*see Chef's Touches*).

3. Preheat the oven to 170°C fan (340°F).

4. Scatter the granulated sugar over a tray or a plate long enough to roll the logs in. When the logs are firm enough, lightly brush each one all over with the beaten egg and roll them one by one in the granulated sugar so they are completely covered. Slice the logs into 2 cm (¾ in) thick discs and lay them flat on a tray lined with baking parchment, spacing them 2 cm (¾ in) apart.

5. Bake for 8–10 minutes, or until nice and golden in colour. Allow to cool completely, then enjoy. They are best eaten on the day, but will keep for 2–3 days in an airtight container.

CHEF'S TOUCHES

When making the shortbread dough, *you can roll it and keep it ready in the refrigerator to be baked any time that day.*

If two shortbread logs is too much for now, *you can keep one in the freezer wrapped in cling film (plastic wrap), ready for another day. Defrost slowly in the refrigerator and bake as above.*

brittany shortbreads

A little shortbread recipe from Brittany. Extremely buttery and crisp on the outside, while slightly soft in the middle. Heaven!

makes 24 shortbread biscuits (*see Chef's Touches*)

PREPARATION TIME
10 minutes

COOKING TIME
15–18 minutes

SPECIAL EQUIPMENT
Mixer with paddle attachment, 12-hole non-stick muffin tray with 6.5 cm (2½ in) cups, 3 cm (1¼ in) deep, piping bag with 1 cm (½ in) plain nozzle

INGREDIENTS

170 g (6 oz/1⅓ cups) plain (all-purpose) flour

4 g (¼ oz) salt

6 g (¼ oz) baking powder

60 g (2 oz) egg yolks

120 g (4¼ oz/½ cup) caster (superfine) sugar

120 g (4¼ oz) unsalted butter, softened

METHOD

1. Preheat the oven to 170°C fan (340°F).
2. In a medium bowl, whisk together by hand the flour, salt and baking powder. Set aside.
3. In the bowl of a stand mixer, whisk together, also by hand, the egg yolks and sugar until pale. Fit the paddle attachment onto the mixer, then add the butter to the yolks and combine on a low speed for a couple of minutes. Add the flour mixture and mix on a low speed for a further 2 minutes, or until fully combined.
4. Using a piping bag with a large plain nozzle, pipe about 20 g (¾ oz) dough into each muffin cup. Bake for 15–18 minutes, or until golden brown. Take out of the oven and allow the shortbreads to cool and firm up for 10–15 minutes. Gently tap them onto a flat tray and let them cool completely.
5. Repeat with the rest of the dough or freeze (*see Chef's Touches*). They are best eaten on the day, but will keep for 2–3 days in an airtight container.

CHEF'S TOUCHES

The recipe makes enough for two rounds of 12 shortbreads, *but you can also roll the second batch into a cylinder, wrap it in cling film (plastic wrap) and store it in the freezer, ready to slice and bake next time.*

You can also bake one large shortbread and use it as the base for a tart-like dessert. *Evenly pipe about 350 g (12 oz) of the mixture into a 20 cm (8 in) cake ring placed on a baking tray lined with baking parchment and bake at 170°C fan (340°F) for about 20 minutes. Let it cool completely before removing the ring.*

palmiers

makes 48 small biscuits

Making palmiers is the art of turning simple puff pastry and caster sugar into a buttery, crispy and caramelised biscuit, which looks like a palm heart. It is all in the technique.

PREPARATION TIME
15 minutes, plus 1 hour resting

COOKING TIME
10 minutes

SPECIAL EQUIPMENT
Baking stone or a heavy baking tray

PLANNING AHEAD
Make the puff pastry (laminated and rested) and make space in the refrigerator.

INGREDIENTS

400 g (14 oz) Quick Puff Pastry (*see page 30*)

200 g (7 oz/generous ¾ cup) caster (superfine) sugar

CHEF'S TOUCHES

The baking parchment placed on top of the palmiers *will help create steam around the biscuits when baking and dissolve the sugar so it caramelises nicely.*

Why not flavour the caster (superfine) sugar *with vanilla seeds or a little ground cinnamon?*

METHOD

ROLLING & SHAPING

1. Ensure the pastry has been laminated and well rested for at least 1 hour in the refrigerator. Give it a single turn *(see page 30, step 4)*. Using roughly 50 g (1¾ oz) sugar, roll the dough in sugar on both sides. Cover the dough with cling film (plastic wrap) and rest in the refrigerator for 1 hour.

2. Unwrap the dough and place it with the seam vertical to you. Roll it out using another 50 g (1¾ oz) sugar until it is about 50 x 30 cm x 3 mm (20 x 12 x ⅛ in) in size. Place the pastry on the work surface with the long side horizontal to you, and pass your hand under the pastry to allow the dough to relax a little and prevent it sticking to the surface. Cut in half vertically to create 2 pieces, each 25 cm (10 in) wide.

3. For each piece, fold the side edges into the middle, leaving a 5 mm (¼ in) gap in the centre. Now fold one side over the other. Place on a tray lined with baking parchment and put in the freezer to firm up for 20 minutes. At this stage, you can cling film and freeze the dough to use later on.

BAKING

4. Preheat the oven to 180°C fan (350°F), with a baking stone or a heavy baking tray inside.

5. Cut the cold palmier dough into 1 cm (½ in) thick slices and toss each piece in the remaining caster sugar. Place each palmier on a flat non-stick tray or a flat tray lined with silicone baking parchment, leaving 4–5 cm (1½–2 in) between each one to allow them to puff up nicely. Cover with a sheet of silicone baking parchment (*see Chef's Touches*).

6. Place the tray of palmiers on the baking stone and bake for 7–8 minutes. Remove from the oven and turn over each palmier, then cover with the parchment once more. Press down each palmier with a large palette knife to flatten. Return the tray to the oven on the hot baking stone and bake for a further 7–8 minutes, or until the biscuits are golden and caramelised. Leave to cool and firm up for 30 minutes before eating. They are best eaten on the day, but will keep for 2–3 days in an airtight container.

viennoiseries

CHAPTER 3

croissants

makes 22–24

The perfect Sunday morning treat.
Nothing feels more French than a freshly
baked croissant.

PREPARATION TIME
20 minutes, plus 1½–2 hours proving

COOKING TIME
12–13 minutes

SPECIAL EQUIPMENT
Pastry brush

PLANNING AHEAD
Allow 4 hours to prepare and rest the croissant dough.

INGREDIENTS

1.1 kg (2 lb 7 oz) ready-to
roll Croissant Dough (*see
page 39*)

2 eggs, beaten, or 100 g
(3½ oz) egg wash (*see
page 70*)

METHOD

ROLLING & SHAPING

1. Roll the rested and cold croissant dough into a
   48–50 x 40–42 cm (19–20 x 16–16½ in) rectangle,
   3–4 mm (⅛–¼ in) thick. Halve lengthways so you have
   two 50 x 20 cm (20 x 8 in) strips. Slice each strip into
   11–12 triangles (*See Chef's Touches and images overleaf*),
   each about 7 cm (2¾ in) wide at the base. Starting at
   the base, roll each triangle into a croissant.

PROVING & BAKING

2. Place each croissant on a cold baking tray lined with
   silicone baking parchment, spacing them 3–4 cm
   (1¼–1½ in) apart. Prove at room temperature for about
   2 hours, or until doubled in volume. Loosely cover the
   croissants with a piece of cling film (plastic wrap) to
   prevent them from drying out. Alternatively, use your
   oven to prove your croissants. (*See Chef's Touches*).
3. Preheat the oven to 210°C fan (410°F).
4. Without deflating the dough, gently brush a thin coat
   of egg wash all over your croissants. Bake for about
   12 minutes, or until nice and golden. Remove from the
   oven and leave to cool for a few minutes before eating
   fresh on the day.

See step-by-step images overleaf

CHEF'S TOUCHES

To prove using your oven, *heat your oven on the lowest setting or
to 40°C fan (100°F) maximum. When it reaches temperature, turn
off the oven and place your tray of croissants inside to prove.
Do not cover with cling film if using this method. Close the door
and prove for about 1¼–1½ hours, or until doubled in volume.
Remove them before preheating the oven for baking.*

To speed up slicing the dough into triangles, *you can stack the
rectangles on top of each other before slicing into triangles (see
images overleaf). Add a little flour before stacking to prevent the
triangles from sticking to each other.*

pain aux raisins

makes 28–30

PREPARATION TIME
30 minutes, plus 1½ hours proving

COOKING TIME
12 minutes

PLANNING AHEAD
Make space in the refrigerator and allow 4 hours to prepare and rest the croissant dough. Also prepare the pastry cream in advance; this can be done a couple of days ahead and kept in the refrigerator.

INGREDIENTS

1.1 kg (2 lb 7 oz) ready-to roll Croissant Dough (*see page 39*)

350 g (12 oz) Pastry Cream (*see page 54*)

240 g (8½ oz/scant 2 cups) sultanas (golden raisins) or raisins

100 g (3½ oz) Sugar Syrup (*see page 70*)

I used to walk out of my way to buy and enjoy the best pain aux raisins in town when I was young. Some bakeries make them with brioche dough, but I have always preferred them made out of a flaky and moreish croissant dough. I hope you will share my view.

METHOD

ROLLING & SHAPING

1. Roll the rested and cold croissant dough into a 70 x 27 cm (28 x 10¾ in) rectangle, 4 mm (¼ in) thick, and position it horizontally in front of you.
2. Whisk the pastry cream until smooth and spread it all over the dough, leaving a 1 cm (½ in) border on the edge closest to you. Sprinkle the sultanas evenly all over the pastry cream and, starting from the top side, tightly roll the dough towards you into a long cylinder.
3. At this stage, you can freeze all or part of your dough (*see Chef's Touches*) or, using a serrated knife, cut your dough cylinder into 2.5 cm (1 in) slices. Line a cold, flat baking tray with silicone baking parchment, and place the slices on it, spacing them 3–4 cm (1¼–1½ in) apart, tucking their loose ends back under to stop the swirls from opening up when baking.

PROVING & BAKING

4. Prove at room temperature for about 2 hours, or until doubled in volume. Loosely cover with a piece of cling film (plastic wrap) to prevent them from drying out. Alternatively, use your oven to prove your pain aux raisins (*see Chef's Touches*).
5. Preheat the oven to 210°C fan (410°F).
6. Bake for about 12 minutes, or until nice and golden. Remove the tray from the oven and brush each swirl with a little bit of sugar syrup straight away to create a lovely shine and extra sweetness. Leave to cool for a few minutes before eating. Enjoy fresh.

CHEF'S TOUCHES

You can also freeze your raw pain aux raisins dough for a few days. *Divide the dough cylinder into three equal logs approximately 20 cm (8 in) long. Wrap each one tightly in cling film (plastic wrap) and freeze nice and flat. The day before you need them, take a roll out of the freezer and keep the cling film on, allowing the dough to defrost overnight in the refrigerator. On the day, cut into 2 cm (¾ in) slices and proceed as above for the proving and baking.*

To prove using your oven, *heat your oven on the lowest setting or to 40°C fan (100°F) maximum. When it reaches temperature, which should not take long, turn off the oven and place your tray of pains aux raisins inside to prove. Close the door and prove for about 1¼–1½ hours, or until doubled in volume. Remove them before preheating the oven for baking.*

chocolate
& pistachio
pain swiss

makes 20—22

PREPARATION TIME
30 minutes, plus 1½–2 hours proving

COOKING TIME
12 minutes

SPECIAL EQUIPMENT
Pastry brush

PLANNING AHEAD
Make space in the refrigerator and allow 4 hours to prepare and rest the croissant dough. Also prepare the pastry cream in advance; it can be done a couple of days ahead and kept in the refrigerator. Finally, get your pistachio paste prepared (if using).

INGREDIENTS

1.1 kg (2 lb 7 oz) ready-to-roll Croissant Dough (*see page 39*)

270 g (9¾ oz) Pastry Cream (*see page 54*), softened (use 350 g/12 oz if not using pistachio paste)

70 g (2½ oz) Pistachio Paste (*see page 60 – optional*)

200 g (7 oz) dark chocolate chips

2 eggs, beaten, or 100 g (3½ oz) Egg Wash (*see page 70*)

100 g (3½ oz) Sugar Syrup (*see page 70*)

I personally prefer this recipe flavoured with pistachio, but you can also leave the pastry cream plain, as it does still taste divine.

METHOD

ROLLING & SHAPING

1. Roll the rested and cold croissant dough into a rectangle about 75 x 27 cm (30 x 10¾ in) and 3–4 mm (⅛–¼ in) thick, and position it horizontally in front of you.

2. Whisk the pastry cream with the pistachio paste until smooth, then spread it all over the rolled dough, leaving a 1 cm (½ in) border on the side closest to you. Sprinkle the chocolate chips all over the cream and then fold the top edge down towards the middle. Fold the bottom edge up to meet it, with the bottom border with no cream overlapping it by 1 cm (½ in). Seal together, pressing down gently with your fingertips. At this stage, you can freeze the dough to bake another time (*see Chef's Touches*).

3. Using a big kitchen knife, cut the dough into 3.5 cm (1½ in) slices and place each pain Swiss on a cold baking tray lined with silicone baking parchment, placing them upside down (so the seam is underneath) and spacing them 4 cm (1½ in) apart.

PROVING & BAKING

4. Prove the pains Swiss at room temperature for about 2 hours, or until doubled in volume. Loosely cover them with a piece of cling film (plastic wrap) to prevent them from drying out. Alternatively, use your oven to prove your pains Swiss (*see Chef's Touches*).

5. Preheat the oven to 210°C fan (410°F).

6. Without deflating the dough, gently brush a thin coat of egg wash all over the top of each pain Swiss. Bake for about 12 minutes, or until nice and golden. Remove from the oven, quickly brush on a thin coat of sugar syrup, and leave to cool for a few minutes before eating fresh.

See step-by-step images overleaf

CHEF'S TOUCHES

You can freeze your raw pains Swiss for a few days. *Wrap the filled and folded dough tightly in cling film (plastic wrap) before slicing, and freeze it nice and flat. The day before you bake, remove it from the freezer and keep the cling film on, allowing the dough to defrost overnight in the refrigerator. On the day, divide into slices and proceed as above for proving and baking.*

To prove using your oven, *heat your oven on the lowest setting or to 40°C fan (100°F) maximum. When it reaches temperature, which should not take long, turn off the oven and place your tray of pains Swiss inside to prove (not covered). Close the door and prove for about 1¼–1½ hours, or until doubled in volume. Remove them before preheating the oven for baking.*

almond croissants

makes 22

In bakeries, they often making these using old croissants that they cut in half, soak in syrup and fill with almond cream: very satisfying, but also quite heavy. This recipe retains some of the flakiness and lightness of the croissant and has a more elegant and flavoursome feel when eating ... I hope you'll enjoy them as much as I do.

PREPARATION TIME
20 minutes, plus 1½–2 hours proving

COOKING TIME
about 12 minutes

SPECIAL EQUIPMENT
Pastry brush

PLANNING AHEAD
Allow 4 hours to prepare and rest the croissant dough.

INGREDIENTS

200 g (7 oz) good-quality marzipan (33% nuts minimum)
1.1 kg (2 lb 7 oz) ready-to-roll Croissant Dough (*see page 39*)

For the glaze
75 ml (2½ fl oz/ 5 tablespoons) orange juice
200 g (7 oz/generous 1½ cups) icing (powdered) sugar
20 ml (1½ tablespoons) Grand Marnier

See step-by-step images overleaf

METHOD

FOR THE MARZIPAN
1. Roll out the marzipan between two sheets of silicone baking parchment to a 30 cm (12 in) square, about 1 mm (1/32 in) thick. Peel off one side of the parchment and cut the marzipan in half, then slice each half into triangles 5 cm (2in) wide and 15 cm (6 in) long. Place the marzipan triangles on a baking sheet in the refrigerator or freezer to firm up a little.

ROLLING & SHAPING
2. Roll out the dough into a 50 x 40cm (20 x 16 in) rectangle, about 4 mm (¼ in) thick. Halve lengthways so you have two 50 x 20 cm (20 x 8 in) strips. Slice each into 11–12 triangles, each about 7 cm (2¾ in) wide at the base.
3. Place a cold triangle of marzipan on top of each triangle of dough. Starting at the base of the triangle, roll each one into a croissant shape.

PROVING & BAKING
4. Place the croissants on a cold baking tray lined with silicone baking parchment, spacing them 3–4 cm (1¼–1½ in) apart. Prove at room temperature for about 2 hours, or until doubled in volume. Loosely cover with cling film (plastic wrap) to prevent them from drying out. Alternatively, use your oven (*see Chef's Touches*).
5. Preheat the oven to 210°C fan (410°F).
6. There's no need to egg-wash those croissants. Bake for about 12 minutes, or until nice and golden. While baking, whisk together the orange juice, icing sugar and Grand Marnier. Brush the mixture all over the croissants straight out of the oven. Leave to cool for at least 20 minutes before eating fresh.

CHEF'S TOUCHES

To prove using your oven, *heat your oven on the lowest setting or to 40°C fan (100°F) maximum. When it reaches temperature, turn off the oven and place your tray of*

croissants (not covered) inside to prove. Close the door and prove for about 1¼–1½ hours, or until doubled in volume. Remove them before preheating the oven for baking.

You can also sprinkle your croissants with toasted flaked (slivered) almonds *for extra texture and a good look.*

brioche
loaf

Allow the beautiful smells of freshly baked brioche into your home and enjoy a taste of France!

◆◇◇ ————————————

serves 8

PREPARATION TIME
15 minutes, plus 2–2½ hours proving

COOKING TIME
35 minutes

SPECIAL EQUIPMENT
26 x 9 cm (10 ½ x 3½ in) loaf tin, 8 cm (3¼ in) deep, pastry brush

PLANNING AHEAD
Allow 4 hours to prepare and rest the dough.

INGREDIENTS

plain (all-purpose) flour, for dusting
400 g (14 oz) chilled Brioche Dough (*see page 42*)
20 g (¾ oz) Egg Wash (*see page 70*)

METHOD

1. On a lightly floured table, divide the cold brioche dough into eight equal portions and roll by hand into round shapes. Leave to rest on the side for a couple of minutes.
2. Meanwhile, line the cake tin (*see Chef's Touches*). Roll the brioche balls a second time, more tightly this time, then place them in the prepared loaf tin, positioning them slightly off-set from each other to fill the tin base. Prove for about 2½ hours, or until the brioche reaches almost to the top of the tin (*see Chef's Touches*).
3. Preheat the oven to 170°C fan (340°F) 20 minutes before baking. Brush the top of the brioche with a thin coat of egg wash, avoiding touching the tin (*see Chef's Touches*).
4. Bake for about 25 minutes, then quickly, using the paper to lift the brioche, take the brioche out of the tin and place it back in the oven on the shelf to bake for a further 10 minutes to dry off the sides of the loaf and prevent it from collapsing.
5. Remove from the oven and allow to cool on a cooling rack before slicing and serving. This is best eaten fresh on the day, but will easily keep for up to 2 days stored in an airtight container. It is great for toasting, too.

CHEF'S TOUCHES

Line the loaf tin with baking parchment, *allowing a couple of centimetres of excess at each end, then folding and pinching the paper on the rim at the tin. This creates two handles that you will use to pull the brioche out of the tin when baked.*

To prove using your oven, *heat your oven on the lowest setting or to 40°C (100°F) fan maximum. When it reaches temperature, which should not take long, turn off the oven and place your brioche inside. Close the door and let the brioche prove until it doubles in volume, which will take about 1¼–1½ hours.*

If the egg wash touches the tin, *the brioche will stick to the tin, which will make it difficult to remove.*

left: Little Brioche Rolls
(see page 108)

right: Brioche Crème
(see page 109)

little brioche rolls

Ideally, you would use the typical non-stick brioche fluted flower-shaped tins for this recipe, but you can also make the dough into simple little rolls if you don't have the tins.

◆ ◇ ◇ ————————————

makes 10

PREPARATION TIME
15 minutes, plus about 2 hours proving

COOKING TIME
10–12 minutes

SPECIAL EQUIPMENT
10 x 6–7 cm (2½ –2 ¾ in) diameter non-stick brioche tins, small pastry brush

PLANNING AHEAD
Make space in the refrigerator and prepare the brioche dough the day before.

INGREDIENTS

oil, for greasing (rapeseed, sunflower or oil spray)
300 g (10½ oz) chilled Brioche Dough (*see page 42*)
20 g (¾ oz) Egg Wash (*see page 70*)

METHOD

1. Lightly brush or spray a very thin coat of oil inside the brioche tins. Divide the brioche dough into ten 30 g (1 oz) portions and roll each one into a round shape. Set aside for a couple of minutes, then roll each ball again so they are nice and neat (*see Chef's Touches*). Place each one inside an individual tin (*see Chef's Touches*). Prove somewhere warm for a couple of hours, or until doubled in volume (*see Chef's Touches*).

2. Preheat the oven to 180°C fan (350°F) 20 minutes before baking. Brush the top of each roll with egg wash (*see Chef's Touches*) and bake for 10–12 minutes.

3. As soon as you remove them from the oven, use a dry cloth to gently tap the brioche out of their tins, then let them cool on a cooling rack. These are best enjoyed fresh, but will last for up to 2 days stored in an airtight container. Once a day old, they are perfect to use for the Polonaise Brioche (*see page 216*).

See recipe image on page 106

CHEF'S TOUCHES

You will warm up the dough first time round with the palm of your hand, *so rolling each ball in two stages makes it less sticky to handle and allows you to form neater balls.*

If not using brioche tins, *place the dough balls on a baking tray lined with baking parchment, evenly spaced, with enough*

room for them to expand when proving and baking.

To prove using the oven, *heat your oven on the lowest setting or to 40 °C fan (100°F) maximum. When it reaches the temperature, which should not take long, turn off the oven off and place your brioche on a tray inside. Close the door*

and let it prove until it doubles in volume, which will take about 1¼–1½ hours.

If the egg wash touches the tin, *the brioche will stick to the tin, which will make it difficult to remove.*

brioche crème

makes 10

PREPARATION TIME
20 minutes, plus 30 minutes resting and 2 hours proving

COOKING TIME
12–15 minutes

SPECIAL EQUIPMENT
Piping bag with medium plain nozzle and a pointy nozzle, pastry brush

PLANNING AHEAD
Make space in the refrigerator and prepare the dough the day before or at least 3 hours in advance. Prepare the pastry cream in advance: it can be done a couple of days ahead and kept in the refrigerator.

INGREDIENTS

400 g (14 oz) chilled Brioche Dough (*see page 42*)

300–350 g (10½–12 oz) Pastry Cream (*see page 54*)

plain flour, for dusting

30 g (1 oz) Egg Wash (*see page 70*)

20 g (¾ oz) Sugar Syrup (*see page 70*)

20–30 g (¾ –1 oz) nibbed sugar

CHEF'S TOUCHES

To prove using the oven: *heat your oven on the lowest setting or to 40°C fan (100°F) maximum. When it reaches the temperature, which should not take long, turn the oven off and place your brioche on a tray inside. Close the door and let it prove until it doubles in volume, which will take about 1¼–1½ hours.*

Silky smooth pastry cream inside brioche: these look absolutely beautiful.

METHOD

1. Divide the brioche dough into ten 40 g (1½ oz) portions and roll each one into a nice, tight round shape. Return to the refrigerator to firm up for 30 minutes.

2. Meanwhile, in a medium bowl, whisk the pastry cream until creamy and smooth. Transfer into a piping bag fitted with a medium plain nozzle. Set aside.

3. On a well-floured table, roll out each individual roll into a 15 cm (6 in) long oval, 8 cm (3¼ in) wide and 2–3 mm thick. Place them back in the refrigerator for 10 minutes to firm up. Once firm, place them back on the lightly floured table, positioning them vertically to you. Pipe an oval of pastry cream, about 12–15 g (½ oz), on to each one, about 3 cm (1¼ in) from the top, as shown on page 110. Fold the top part of the dough over the pastry cream and seal it in tightly with your fingers.

4. Using a paring knife, make four or five equally spaced marks in the bottom part of the dough, coming down from the base of the sealed cream, and cut them to create six strips. Roll the sealed pastry cream over these strips, as shown overleaf. Repeat with the remaining dough and place each brioche roll on a baking tray, ensuring that the seams end up under the brioche and the dough strips sit nicely over the tops. Prove in a warm place for a couple of hours, or until doubled in volume (*see Chef's Touches*).

5. Preheat the oven to 170°C fan (340°F) 20 minutes before baking. Lightly brush just the top of the brioche dough strips with a bit of egg wash and bake for 12–15 minutes until nice and golden. Remove from the oven and immediately lightly brush the brioche with a little sugar syrup, then quickly sprinkle over the nibbed sugar. Allow to cool.

6. Using a pointy nozzle or a skewer, prick a hole in one end of each brioche, or use a gap where some of the pastry cream may have come out during baking, and fill them with the remaining pastry cream. These are best enjoyed fresh, but will last for up to 2 days stored in an airtight container.

See recipe image on page 107, and step-by-step images on pages 110–111

for the brioche crème

candied fruit brioche

serves 8

PREPARATION TIME
15 minutes, plus 2 hours proving

COOKING TIME
40–45 minutes

SPECIAL EQUIPMENT
20 cm (8 in) cake ring or cake tin, 5–6 cm (2–2½ in) deep, pastry brush

PLANNING AHEAD
Prepare the brioche up to a day ahead.

INGREDIENTS

butter, for greasing
200 g (7 oz) Pastry Cream
  (*see page 54*)
Plain (all-purpose) flour,
  for dusting
500 g (1 lb 2 oz) chilled
  Brioche Dough
  (*see page 42*)

110 g (3¾ oz) candied fruit
  cubes (you can also use
  sultanas or raisins)
20 g (¾ oz) Sugar Syrup (*see
  page 70*)
4–5 glacé cherries

A colourful brioche for sharing ... enjoy.

METHOD

1. Lightly butter the inside of the cake ring and line it with a band of baking parchment Place the ring on a flat baking tray lined with baking parchment and set aside.

2. In a medium bowl, whisk the pastry cream until smooth and creamy. On a floured table, using a rolling pin, roll the brioche dough to roughly the size of an A4 sheet of paper (30 x 22–25 cm/12 x 8½–10 in) and position it in a landscape orientation in front of you.

3. Using a palette knife, spread the pastry cream all over the dough, then sprinkle over the candied fruit. Roll the dough tightly towards you into a log, then using a big knife, divide the roll into ten equal slices. Arrange each slice on its side, inside the prepared cake ring, finishing in the centre. Top with the glacé cherries. Allow to prove for a couple of hours in a warm place, or until it doubles in volume (*see Chef's Touches*).

4. Preheat the oven to 170°C fan (340°F) 20 minutes before baking. Bake for about 30 minutes. Carefully remove the cake ring with a dry cloth and then return the brioche to the oven to then return the brioche to the oven to bake for a further 10–15 minutes to dry off the crust. Remove from the oven and immediately brush the top lightly with sugar syrup, or alternatively with a warm lemon icing (*see page 166*). Leave to cool completely on a cooling rack before eating. Stored in an airtight container at room temperature, this will keep for up to 3 days.

CHEF'S TOUCHES

To prove using the oven, *heat your oven on the lowest setting or to 40 °C (100 °F) fan maximum. When it reaches the* *temperature, which should not take long, turn off the oven and place your brioche on a tray to prove inside. Close the door and* *let it prove until it doubles in volume, which will take about 1¼–1½ hours.*

passion fruit doughnuts

This recipe has been kindly given to me by one of my colleagues, little Nick, who baked it for charity during lockdown.

makes 12

PREPARATION TIME
Curd 20 minutes; doughnuts 25 minutes, plus 1 hour proving

COOKING TIME
6 minutes

SPECIAL EQUIPMENT
Hand blender, deep-fat fryer or a pan with oil (about 5 cm/2 in deep), temperature probe, strainer ladle or similar, piping bag with 6–8 mm (¼–⅜ in) plain nozzle

PLANNING AHEAD
Make the passion fruit curd the night before.

INGREDIENTS

For the passion fruit curd
60 g (2 oz) peeled fresh
  mango, diced
3–4 fresh passion fruit
  (about 60 g/2 oz flesh and
  juice)
45 g (1½ oz) egg yolks
55 g (2 oz ¼ cup) caster
  (superfine) sugar
20 g (¾ oz/1½ tablespoons)
  cornflour (cornstarch)
150 g (5½ oz/scant ⅔ cup)
  whipping cream
10 g (½ oz/2 teaspoons)
  lemon juice
60 g (2 oz) unsalted butter,
  at room temperature

For the doughnuts
320 g (10¾ oz/2½ cups)
  strong bread flour, plus
  extra for dusting
10 g (½ oz) fast-action dried
  yeast or 20 g (¾ oz) fresh
  yeast
25 g (1 oz/scant
  2 tablespoons) caster
  (superfine) sugar
3 g (½ teaspoon) salt
150 g (5½ oz/scant ⅔ cup)
  whole milk
50 g (1¾ oz) unsalted butter
50 g (1¾ oz) egg, beaten

For rolling the doughnuts
100 g (3½ oz/scant ½ cup)
  caster (superfine) sugar
Zest of ¼ lime

METHOD

MAKING THE CURD
1. Place the diced mango in a small jug. Cut the passion fruits in half and, using a spoon, scoop out the juice and seeds and add to the diced mango. Blitz together with a hand blender until smooth, and pass the purée through a sieve to remove the passion fruit seeds (this should yield about 120 g/4¼ oz purée – *see Chef's Touches*).

2. In a medium bowl, whisk together the egg yolks, sugar and cornflour. In a medium saucepan over a low heat, warm the whipping cream with the fruit, then pour it over the yolk mixture and whisk together. Transfer back into the pan and bring to the boil for 2 minutes over a medium heat, whisking continuously to thicken. Remove from the heat and add the lemon juice. Transfer into a clean medium bowl and leave to cool until lukewarm.

3. Using a hand blender, blitz in the butter. Cover the top of the curd with cling film (plastic wrap), touching the curd, and keep in the refrigerator until needed.

MAKING THE DOUGHNUTS
4. Place all the dry ingredients in a large bowl, keeping the salt away from the yeast (*see Chef's Touches*). Make a well in the centre.

5. In a small over a medium heat, warm the milk until lukewarm, then melt in the butter. Whisk in the beaten egg and pour this mixture into the well in the dry ingredients. Mix all the ingredients together by hand and turn out onto a floured surface. Knead for 10 minutes.

6. Transfer the dough into an large oiled bowl and leave in a warm place to prove for 15–20 minutes, loosely covered. Transfer the dough back on to the table and divide into twelve 50 g (1¾ oz) portions. Roll into balls and place each one on a tray lined with baking parchment to prove for 30–40 minutes, or until doubled in size.

CHEF'S TOUCHES

The purée can be replaced with 120 g (4¼ oz) passion fruit and mango juice, *as long as it is not too sweet.*

The salt will kill the yeast *if placed in direct contact with it.*

7. Meanwhile, preheat the oil for deep-frying to 165°C (330°F). In a large bowl, combine the caster sugar and lime zest, ready to toss the doughnuts in.

8. When fully proved, deep-fry the doughnuts, 2–3 at a time, for 3 minutes on each side, or until nice and golden, flipping them over using a strainer ladle or similar. Drain off the excess oil and let them stand on paper towels for a few minutes. Once cooled, toss them in the sugar and lime and, using a small pointy nozzle or the tip of a skewer, make a hole on one side of each doughnut into the centre, wiggling around a little to hollow out. Transfer the cold passion fruit curd into a piping bag fitted with a 6–8 mm (¼–⅜ in) plain nozzle and fill each doughnut with about 30 g (1 oz) curd. Enjoy!

chelsea buns

A flaky version of the traditional bun, baked in a tray.

makes 8–10

PREPARATION TIME
1¼ hours resting, 1½ hours proving

COOKING TIME
25 minutes

SPECIAL EQUIPMENT
22 cm (8½ in) square baking tray about 4–5 cm (1½ in) deep, temperature probe (ideally)

PLANNING AHEAD
Soak the fruits 1–2 hours in advance to allow good flavour absorption.

INGREDIENTS

For soaking the fruit
50 g (1¾ oz/3½ tablespoons) water
50 g (1¾ oz/¼ cup) caster (superfine) sugar
25 g (1 oz/1½ tablespoons) mixed peel
75 g (2½ oz/⅔ cup) sultanas (golden raisins)

For the dough
250 g (9 oz/2 cups) strong bread flour
55 g (2 oz) unsalted butter, plus 75 g (2½ oz) butter, softened, for the single turn
4 g (¼ oz) salt

110 g (3¾ oz/½ cup) full-fat milk
25 g (1 oz) fresh yeast
1 small egg, beaten
40 g (2½ oz/¼ cup) light soft brown sugar

For the spiced butter
5 g (¼ oz) ground mixed spice
25 g (1 oz) unsalted butter, softened

METHOD

SOAKING THE FRUIT

1. In a saucepan, bring the water and sugar to a quick boil and add the dried fruit. Take off the heat and leave to soak for 1–2 hours.

MAKING & BAKING THE BUNS

2. In a medium bowl, crumb together by hand the flour, butter and salt. Warm the milk in a saucepan or in a bowl in the microwave until it is lukewarm (maximum 35–40°C/95–104°F), then add the fresh yeast to dissolve. Add the beaten egg, then add this mixture to the bowl with the flour and butter and mix to make a dough. Gently knead the dough on the table for 10 minutes, then prove in the bowl for 30 minutes.

3. Meanwhile, prepare the spiced butter. In a bowl, whisk together the butter and mixed spice. Set aside.

4. Line the deep baking tray with baking parchment (*see Chef's Touches*).

5. Roll out the rested dough to about 30 x 20 cm (12 x 8 in).

6. Drain the soaked fruit and save the liquid for the glaze. Using a palette knife, spread the 75 g (2½ oz) softened butter over two-thirds of the length of the dough and give it one single turn (*see page 30, step 4*).

7. Place back in the refrigerator to rest for about 15 minutes, then roll out the dough to a rectangle until about 26 x 24 cm (10½ x 9½ in) and about 4–5 mm (¼ in) thick. Spread the spiced butter all over the dough, leaving a 2 cm (¾ in) gap at the bottom. Sprinkle over the brown sugar, then the drained mixed fruit. Starting from the top, tightly roll the dough into a long cylinder. Using a serrated knife, divide it into 8–10 slices, 3 cm (1¼ in) wide. Place each slice on its side in a baking tray, evenly spaced out. Prove in a warm place for about 1 hour, or until doubled in size.

8 Meanwhile, preheat the oven to 200°C fan (400°F). When proved, bake the buns in the middle of the oven for about 25 minutes.

9. Remove from the oven and immediately brush the reserved fruit soaking liquid all over the top of the buns. Allow to cool for 5 minutes, then lift out of the tin using the paper 'handles' created when lining the tray. Transfer onto a cooling rack to cool fully. These are best enjoyed fresh, but kept in an airtight container will last for up to 2 days.

Make sure the milk is lukewarm and not hotter than 40°C (104°F), *or the heat will kill the yeast and it will not work.*

Line the baking tray with baking parchment, *with a couple of centimetres of excess on both sides, folding and pinching the paper at the rim of the baking tray.*

This will create two handles that you can use to pull the buns out of the tray when baked.

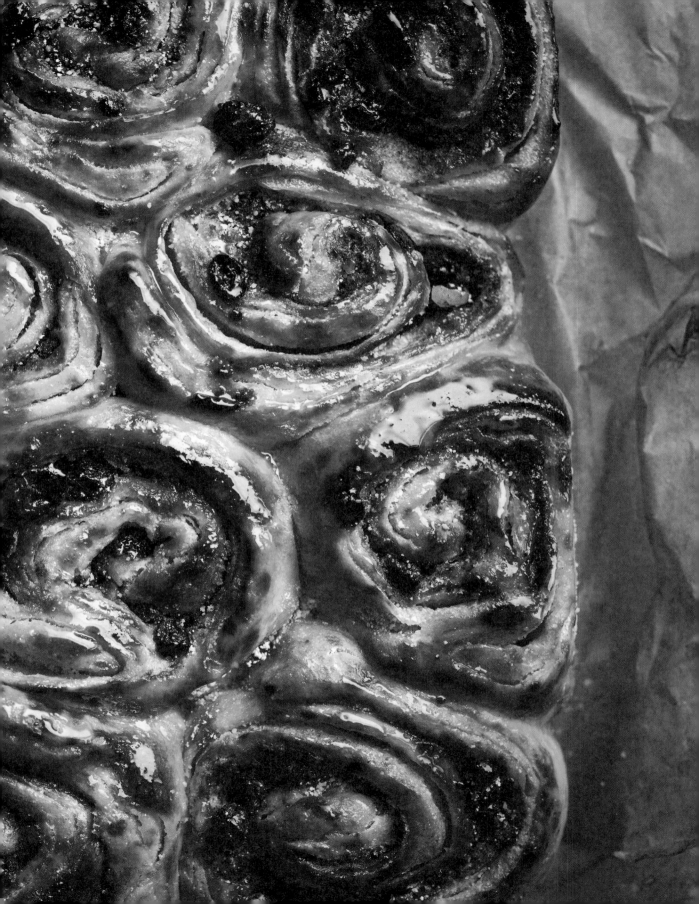

apple kouign-amann

makes 15

This apple kouign-amann is simply my favourite viennoiserie! Originally a plain butter cake from Brittany, I've added the apple element to cut through the richness of what was a very sweet and fatty pastry. It also made a lot of sense to use the orchard apples on our doorstep.

PREPARATION TIME
40 minutes, plus 5–6 hours resting and 2½ hours proving

COOKING TIME
16–18 minutes

SPECIAL EQUIPMENT
15 x 7.5 cm (3 in) foil tins, 3 cm (1¼ in) deep, piping bag with 6 mm (¼ in) plain nozzle, mixer with dough hook attachment, temperature probe

PLANNING AHEAD
This recipe can be made in one day but ideally gets prepared over two: make the dough and do the lamination on day one, before proving, baking and finishing the day after. Prepare the apple compôte in advance.

INGREDIENTS

500 g (1 lb 2 oz) homemade
Apple Compôte (*see page 72*)

For the dough
400 g (14 oz/3¼ cups)
strong bread flour, plus
extra for dusting
170 g (6 oz/¾ cup) chilled
water
½ egg, beaten
7 g (¼ oz) salt
20 g (¾ oz) fresh yeast
40 g (1½ oz/scant 3
tablespoons) caster
(superfine) sugar
6 g (¼ oz) vanilla extract

For the lamination
250 g (9 oz) good-quality
unsalted butter (82% fat)
40 g (1½ oz) salted butter,
softened
20 g (¾ oz/1 tablespoon
+ 2 teaspoons) granulated
sugar
20 g (¾ oz/1 tablespoon +
2 teaspoons) demerara
sugar

For lining the tins
30 g (1 oz/2 tablespoons)
caster (superfine) sugar
30 g (1 oz/2 tablespoons)
demerara sugar
40 g (1½ oz) unsalted butter,
softened

METHOD

FOR THE DOUGH
1. In a mixer with the dough hook attachment, mix all the dough ingredients for 5 minutes on a low speed. Increase the speed to medium for about 10 minutes, or until the dough is nicely worked out and reaches a temperature of about 27 °C (81 °F). Ball the dough on the table and place it on a cold tray lined with baking parchment. Flatten it gently and cover it with cling film (plastic wrap). Place the tray in the freezer for about 20 minutes to cool the dough, then transfer it to the refrigerator for a minimum of 3 hours, or overnight.

LINING THE TINS
2. In a small bowl, combine both sugars. Brush the softened butter inside the tins, then coat with the mixed sugars. Reserve in the refrigerator.

LAMINATING THE DOUGH
3. Between two sheets of baking parchment, roll out the 250 g (9 oz) unsalted butter into a rectangle about 21 x 16 cm (8¼ x 6¼ in) and 6 mm (¼ in) thick. Roll out the dough to about 32 x 21cm/12¾ x 8¼ in and place the rolled-out butter in the centre of the dough. Fold the dough over the butter towards the middle and give it two single turns (*see page 30, step 4*). Cover with cling film and leave to rest for 1 hour on a flat tray in the refrigerator.
4. After 1 hour, remove the dough from the refrigerator and roll it out as if you were going to give it another turn. Before folding, spread the softened salted butter over the dough using a palette knife. Combine the both sugars and cover the butter. Fold to finish the single turn. Leave the dough to rest in the refrigerator for another hour, as before.
5. On a well-floured table, roll the cold dough into a rectangle measuring about 45 x 27cm (17¾ x 10¾ in) and about 3–4 mm (⅛–¼ in) thick. Using a kitchen knife, cut the dough into 15 x 9 cm (3½ in) squares.

Fold the corners of each into the centre and press gently to hold the points in place. Place each folded square face down into the prepared tins.

BAKING & FINISHING

6. Prove the kouign-amann in a warm place for about 2½ hours. Thirty minutes before baking, preheat the oven to 175 °C fan (340°F).

7. Bake the kouign-amann for 16–18 minutes, turning the tray halfway through, until nicely caramelised and golden brown. Remove from the oven and release the kouign-amann from the tins straight away by flipping the tins upside down, then flip the kouign-amann again and place them caramel-side down on a flat tray lined with baking parchment. Leave to cool completely at room temperature (*see Chef's Touches*).

8. Make a hole in the back of each kouign-amann with a small pointy nozzle or a wooden skewer, and pipe about 30 g (1 oz) apple compôte into each one. Present your kouign-amann caramelised side up on the serving dish or in a basket.

CHEF'S TOUCHES

Lamination *is the technique used in puff pastry and croissant dough to trap the butter inside the dough and fold it together several times to achieve a nice flaky structure. This will help the* *caramel to set flat and not collapse, and help the bakes look sharp when presented.*

pies & tarts

CHAPTER 4

apricot tarte boulangère

serves 4–6

PREPARATION TIME
15 minutes

COOKING TIME
40–45 minutes

PLANNING AHEAD
Prepare the puff pastry and the pastry cream in advance. Keep some sponge trimmings that you may have hanging around in your kitchen.

This apricot tart is inspired by the bakeries in France. In the bakeries back in the day, there were always spare sponge trimmings flying around from all the cakes that had been made, so one way to avoid food waste and ultimately absorb the extra moisture coming out of the apricots while baking was to sprinkle some sponge crumbs into the tart base before the apricots were added.

INGREDIENTS

For the base
18 cm (7 in) rolled-out disc of Puff Pastry (*see page 30*), 3.5 mm (⅛ in) thick

For the fruit
12 tinned or fresh apricot halves
20 g (¾ oz/1 tablespoon + 2 teaspoons) caster (superfine) sugar (if using fresh apricots)
5 g (¼ oz/1 teaspoon) lemon juice (if using fresh apricots)

For the filling
60 g (2 oz) Pastry Cream (*see page 54*)
2 tablespoons sponge trimmings (*see Chef's Touches*)

For the finishing touches
50 g (1¾ oz) apricot jam
1–2 sprigs of lavender, (*see Chef's Touches*)
20 g (¾ oz/2¼ tablespoons) icing (powdered) sugar, for dusting

METHOD

1. Preheat the oven to 170°C fan (340°F).
2. Place the disc of puff pastry on a baking tray lined with baking parchment. If using tinned apricots, drain them and set aside. If using fresh apricots, *see Chef's Touches*.
3. In a small bowl, whisk the pastry cream, then use a spoon to spread it on top of the puff pastry disc, leaving a border of 2–3 cm (¾–1¼ in) around the edge. Crumble and sprinkle over the sponge trimmings with your fingers. Cut the apricot halves into quarters, except for one. Arrange the apricot quarters, and line the rest, cut-side up on top of the pastry cream in a flower shape, starting at the edges and continuing towards the centre, overlapping them. Finish by placing the reserved apricot half, also cut-side up, in the middle. Bake for 40–45 minutes until the puff pastry is cooked through. Allow to cool completely.
4. In a small pan over a medium heat, combine the apricot jam with the picked lavender flowers (*see Chef's Touches*). Bring it to a quick boil to melt, then brush it all over the apricots. Using a small sieve, sprinkle the edges of the tart with the icing sugar. This is best enjoyed fresh, but when stored in an airtight container in the refrigerator will last for up to 2 days.

CHEF'S TOUCHES

If using fresh fruit, *combine the lemon juice and the sugar in a medium bowl, then add the fresh apricot halves and toss.*

You only need the blue tips of the lavender, *not the stems or the leaves, which will make the flavour too strong.*

my apple pie

serves 8

PREPARATION TIME
20 minutes, plus 30 minutes resting

COOKING TIME
1 hour

SPECIAL EQUIPMENT
1 x 20 cm (8 in) cake ring, 4 cm (1½ in) deep

PLANNING AHEAD
Make the apple compote the day before.

For the dough
190 g (6¾ oz/1½ cups) plain
  (all-purpose) flour, plus
  extra for dusting
2 g (½ teaspoon) baking
  powder
100 g (3½ oz/scant ½ cup)
  caster (superfine) sugar
115 g (4 oz) unsalted butter,
  chilled, plus extra for
  greasing
1 egg
5 g (1 teaspoon) vanilla
  extract

For the filling
150 g (5½ oz) Apple
  Compôte (*see page 72*)
4 medium apples (700 g/
  1 lb 9 oz) (I use Braeburn)
2 teaspoons caster
  (superfine) sugar
¼ teaspoon ground
  cinnamon

For the topping
1 medium (170 g/6 oz)
  Braeburn apple, peeled,
  cored and sliced into 12
  segments

CHEF'S TOUCHES

I think it is quicker *to mix the dough by hand.*

When hot, *the pastry is extremely fragile and will not be able to hold the apple mixture inside. Let it cool as much as possible to firm up.*

This simple recipe is inspired by a Swedish apple dessert I recreated for one of our guests at Le Manoir. I prefer using Braeburn apples, but if these are not available, choose an apple which does not break down too much and has a good flavour, like a Granny Smith or a Royal Gala. However, there are many more apple varieties out there which would work and that you may want to try.

METHOD

MAKING THE DOUGH
1. Whisk together the flour, baking powder and sugar. By hand, rub in the diced cold butter until a crumb-like texture. Add the egg and vanilla extract. Combine into a dough (*see Chef's Touches*). Push the dough against the surface once, to ensure all the ingredients are fully incorporated.
2. Split the dough into two pieces, 300 g (10½ oz) for the base of the pie and 170 g (6 oz) for the lid. Flatten and place on a cold tray lined with baking parchment and chill in the refrigerator for 30 minutes.

MAKING THE PIE
3. On a floured surface, roll out the 300 g (10½ oz) piece of dough into a 26 cm (10½ in) diameter disc, 3 mm (⅛ in) thick. Rub the cake ring with a little chunk of butter to prevent the dough sticking, then place it on a flat baking tray lined with baking parchment. Line the ring with the pastry disc to make the pie base, making sure the dough comes up the sides, just about overlapping the ring.
4. Roll out the 170 g (6 oz) piece of dough into a 3 mm (⅛ in) thick disc, about the same diameter as the ring, and transfer to the refrigerator.
5. Spread the apple compôte evenly all over the base of the pie with a spoon. Peel and core the apples. Using a coarse grater, grate the apples into the pie case, pressing down with your hand to level them. Combine the sugar with the cinnamon and sprinkle half of this mixture all over the grated apples. Fold the excess pastry back in and over the grated apples, just over the edges. The pie will now be shallower than the ring. Cover the top with the cold disc of pastry, making sure to seal the edges.
6. On top of the pie, elegantly fan out the 12 apple segments in a flower shape and sprinkle all over with the remaining cinnamon sugar.

BAKING

7. Preheat the oven to 170°C fan (340°F).
8. Bake the pie for 30 minutes, then rotate the tray to ensure even baking and bake for another 30 minutes. Remove from the oven and leave to cool for at least

15 minutes to allow the dough to set (*see Chef's Touches*).

9. When firm enough, slide the pie (with the ring and baking parchment) onto a cooling rack and remove the ring to finish cooling. This is best enjoyed fresh, but will keep for up to 2 days in an airtight container.

rhubarb &
custard tart

serves 6–8

For this tart, you can use either forced rhubarb in the early part of the year, which is pink, tender and sweet, or the typical garden rhubarb from late spring onwards, although you may need to add a little more sugar when marinating the stems. For me, both are delicious.

PREPARATION TIME
20 minutes, plus 1 hour 10 minutes resting

COOKING TIME
25 minutes to blind-bake the tart case, 8 minutes for the rhubarb and 15 minutes to bake the tart as a whole

SPECIAL EQUIPMENT
20 cm (8 in) tart ring, 2 cm (¾ in) deep, plus a blowtorch if you have one

PLANNING AHEAD
To save energy, you can prepare and macerate the rhubarb 1 hour before finishing the tart. That way, you can cook it while preheating the oven and preparing the blind-baked shortcrust pastry case.

INGREDIENTS

1 x 20 cm (8 in) blind-baked
   Shortcrust Pastry Tart
   Case (*see page 28*)
icing (powdered) sugar, for
   dusting

For the rhubarb
380 g (13 oz) trimmed
   forced rhubarb

100 g (3½ oz/scant ½ cup)
   caster (superfine) sugar

For the tart filling
1 egg
15 g (½ oz) caster (superfine)
   sugar
1 lemon
65 g (2¼ oz/¼ cup) double
   (heavy) cream

CHEF'S TOUCHES

Partially cooking the rhubarb *allows it to release some of its juices now and not in the tart case later, as that would make the case go soft could cause the egg mixture to split.*

METHOD

FOR THE RHUBARB
1. Wash the rhubarb stems and cut them into 2 cm (¾ in) chunks (if using garden rhubarb, you may also want to peel off the big shoots if the skin feels a bit stringy). Place them into a small baking tray and scatter over the sugar, then cover and leave to macerate for about 1 hour.
2. Preheat the oven to 160°C fan (320°F).
3. Transfer the rhubarb to the oven and cook for about 8 minutes, or 10–12 minutes if using garden rhubarb. Remove from the oven and leave to rest on the side for 10 minutes to finish cooking through. Tip into a large sieve over a bowl to drain and collect the cooking liquor (*see Chef's Touches*).

FILLING & BAKING
4. In a medium bowl, whisk together the egg, sugar and a very small amount of lemon zest. Add 40 g (1½ oz/2½ tablespoons) of the reserved rhubarb cooking liquor and the cream.
5. Increase the oven temperature to 170°C fan (340°F).
6. With a spoon, arrange the drained rhubarb chunks nicely all over the blind-baked tart case. Cover the rhubarb with the egg mixture, making sure it reaches up to the edges of the case. Bake for 14–15 minutes, or until the custard cream sets on top. Remove the tart from the oven and leave to cool for at least 20 minutes. Using a small sieve, generously dust icing sugar all over the tart and slightly caramelise the centre with a blowtorch, if desired, before serving. This is best enjoyed on the day, but will keep for up to 2 days stored in an airtight container.

millionaire's chocolate tart

serves 6–8

This is one of the first desserts I actually put together during lockdown. I had a little bit of soft caramel in my refrigerator from another dish which I did not know what to do with, so I made a very crumbly sablé pastry, adding the soft and gooey caramel with a moreish dark chocolate cream on top – *et voilà*, success! It went down a treat with all the family.

PREPARATION TIME
1 hour, plus 3 hours setting

COOKING TIME
12–14 minutes for the tart case

SPECIAL EQUIPMENT
20 cm (8 in) tart ring, 2 cm (¾ in) deep, piping bag with an 8 mm (⅜ in) plain nozzle, thermometer probe

PLANNING AHEAD
Prepare and blind-bake the pastry tart case.

INGREDIENTS

1 x 20 cm (8 in) blind-baked Sablé Pastry Tart Case (*see page 24*)
100 g (3½ oz) Dark Chocolate Curls (*see page 64*)
icing (powdered) sugar, for dusting
cocoa powder, for dusting (*optional*)

For the soft caramel
150 g (5½ oz/scant ⅔ cup) whipping cream
pinch of sea salt

100 g (3½ oz/scant ½ cup) caster (superfine) sugar
100 g (3½ oz) glucose syrup
40 g (1½ oz) lightly salted butter, diced

For the chocolate cream
160 g (5¾ oz/⅔ cup) whipping cream
60 g (2 oz/¼ cup) whole milk
1 egg, beaten
155 g (5½ oz) 70% good-quality dark chocolate

CHEF'S TOUCHES

Using a deep pan and adding the hot cream in batches *will help to prevent the mixture boiling over.*

When the caramel starts to smoke, *it becomes extremely hot and becomes very bitter.*

METHOD

MAKING THE CARAMEL

1. In a small pan, heat the cream with the salt over a low heat and set aside.
2. In a deep, medium saucepan (*see Chef's Touches*), make a dry caramel by melting the sugar with the glucose, mixing it with a spatula. Cook until it is a caramel brown colour, making sure you take it off the heat before it starts to smoke (*see Chef's Touches*). Carefully pour in the hot cream in three batches, whisking it into the caramel. Return the pan to the heat and bring it back to a quick boil, then remove from the heat and whisk in the diced butter. Pour into a flat container and leave to cool and thicken for 30–40 minutes.
3. Pour half the caramel into the baked tart case and spread it out, then leave to set in the refrigerator for 1 hour. Reserve the rest to decorate.

FOR THE CHOCOLATE CREAM

4. In a medium saucepan, bring the cream and milk to the boil. Pour this into a bowl with the beaten egg and whisk to combine. Break the chocolate into pieces in another bowl, then pour half of the cream mixture over the top and stir gently until smooth. Add the remaining cream mixture and stir again.
5. Pour the chocolate cream into the tart case over the set caramel and return the tart to the refrigerator to set for at least a couple of hours.

ASSEMBLING

6. Using a piping bag with a 8 mm (⅜ in) nozzle, pipe the remaining soft caramel over the tart in a large spiral. Top with the dark chocolate curls and, with a small sieve, dust with a little icing sugar and cocoa powder. Enjoy. This is best eaten on the day, but will keep for up to 2 days in an airtight container stored in the refrigerator.

gâteau basque

serves 8

PREPARATION TIME
45 minutes

COOKING TIME
40 minutes, plus 1–2 hours resting time

SPECIAL EQUIPMENT
Mixer with paddle attachment and a 22 cm/8½ in loose-bottom fluted non-stick tart tin, 3cm (11/4in) deep with removable base

PLANNING AHEAD
Brew a bag of red berry herbal tea in a jug for 3 minutes. Remove the teabag and pour 150 ml (5 fl oz/scant ⅔ cup) of the hot brew over 170 g (6 oz/scant ½ cup) roughly chopped dried prunes to soak them. Cover with cling film (plastic wrap) for about 15 minutes. Drain the prunes and marinate them with a dash of Armagnac.

INGREDIENTS

For the dough
225 g (8 oz) plain
  (all-purpose) flour, plus
  extra for dusting
5 g (1 teaspoon) baking
  powder
155 g (5½ oz) unsalted
  butter, plus extra for
  greasing
150 g (5½ oz) caster
  (superfine) sugar
1 small egg, plus 1 yolk
½ vanilla pod
3 g (½ teaspoon) salt

For the pastry cream filling
¾ vanilla pod
310 g (11 oz/1¼ cups) whole
  milk
3 egg yolks
25 g (1 oz/¼ cup) cornflour
  (cornstarch)
80 g (2¾ oz) caster
  (superfine) sugar
30 g (1 oz) unsalted butter,
  diced
20 g (¾ oz/1½ tablespoons)
  dark rum
soaked dried prunes (see
  planning ahead)

For the glaze
1 egg yolk, beaten

A beautiful French classic originating from the Basque region in France, which my former head pastry chef at the Ritz Hotel in Paris gave me to try over the lockdown. Thank you, Christian. The classic recipe is normally made using cherry jam, but with this one I am using dried prunes, which was what I had at the time. I think they work well too. The gâteau is usually enjoyed as a dessert, but also in the afternoon on a well-deserved tea break.

METHOD

MAKING THE DOUGH

1. Sift together the flour and the baking powder. In the mixer with the paddle attachment, cream together the butter and sugar on a low speed. Add the egg and the extra yolk, along with the seeds of the vanilla pod and the salt. Add the sifted flour mixture and combine for a couple of minutes until smooth.

2. Transfer the dough onto a stretched-out piece of cling film (plastic wrap) and fold over into a square-ish parcel about 3 cm (1¼ in) deep. Place in the refrigerator to rest for at least 1–2 hours.

FOR THE PASTRY CREAM FILLING

3. In a medium saucepan over a medium heat, scrape the seeds of the vanilla pod into the milk, then add the pod and bring to the boil.

4. Meanwhile, in a bowl, whisk together the yolks, cornflour and sugar. As soon as the vanilla milk boils, take it off the heat and pour one-quarter of it over the yolk mixture and whisk rapidly. Pour this back into the pan with the milk and whisk continuously. Place back over a medium heat, and continue whisking until the mixture starts thickening. Take the pan off the heat and continue to whisk until smooth. When thickened and smooth return to the heat and bring to a quick boil. Take off the heat, remove the vanilla pod with a fork and whisk in the butter and rum. Leave to cool. Once cool, whisk until smooth and set aside.

Recipe continued overleaf

BUILDING & BAKING

5. Preheat the oven to 165°C fan (330°F).

6. Lightly butter the inside of the tart tin using your fingers. Take the dough out of the refrigerator, cut away one-third and set in the refrigerator for the lid. On a well-floured surface, roll the remaining two-thirds of the dough into a 30 cm (12 in) diameter disc about 4 mm (¼ in) thick, and use this to line the tart mould. The dough will overlap the mould slightly.

7. Evenly spread the chopped, soaked prunes across the base of the tart and cover with the pastry cream filling. Level the cream filling with a spoon and fold the dough excess back over the cream to give the lid something to stick to later on.

8. Take the remaining one-third of dough and roll it into a disc of the same diameter as the tart mould. Place the disc on the top of the cream. Level, pressing carefully with your hand, and trim the edges by, applying gentle pressure with a rolling pin. Brush the top of the pie all over with the beaten egg yolk and, using gentle pressure, score three evenly spaced fork-mark lines across the pie, followed by a further three on a diagonal to create a diamond pattern.

9. Bake in the middle of the oven for 30–35 minutes, or until golden brown. Remove from the oven and leave to cool completely and set before trying to take it out of the tin (*see Chef's Touches*).

10. The gâteau should be slightly crispy on the outside but with a soft, almost spongy, texture on the inside. I hope you enjoy it as much as I did! Best eaten fresh, though stored in an airtight container it will last for up to 2 days.

CHEF'S TOUCHES

When hot, *the pastry is extremely fragile and will not be able to hold the mixture inside. Letting it cool completely will firm up the pie crust and make it possible to remove from the mould.*

You can replace *the soaked dried prunes with a slightly acidic cherry compote or jam. Alternatively, my daughter Juju really liked it when I used a good-quality or homemade raspberry jam.*

tarte tatin

serves 6

PREPARATION TIME
15 minutes

COOKING TIME
1 hour 25 minutes–1 hour 40 minutes

SPECIAL EQUIPMENT
20 x 10 cm (8 x 4 in) non-stick Charlotte mould, or a similar size ovenproof saucepan

PLANNING AHEAD
Prepare and roll out the puff pastry. You can also use store-bought puff pastry.

INGREDIENTS

70 g (2½ oz) unsalted butter
150 g (5½ oz/⅔ cup) caster (superfine) sugar
1.2–1.3 kg (2 lb 12 oz–3 lb) Braeburn apples (about 150–170 g/5½–6 oz each)

250 g (9 oz) Quick Puff Pastry (*see page 30*), rolled into a 21 cm (8¼ in) disc, 3 mm (⅛ in) thick
vanilla ice cream or crème fraîche, to serve

My go-to apple for this recipe is a Braeburn, which cooks very well while holding its shape; it compacts well together and has a great flavour. Different types of apple may work, such as Cox's orange pippin, Chantecler, golden delicious or Granny Smith, but the cooking time and end result will differ for each variety.

METHOD

MAKING & BAKING

1. In a small saucepan over a low heat, melt the butter and sugar together. Using a wooden spoon, stir to combine, and gradually increase the heat and cook until you have a smooth, light brown caramel (*see Chef's Touches*). Quickly transfer the caramel into the Charlotte mould and continue stirring with the wooden spoon until it stops cooking. Set aside to cool.

2. Preheat the oven to 170°C fan (340°F). Peel and core the apples and cut them in half (*see Chef's Touches*). Arrange them in the mould, with the base part of the apple against the side of the mould (*see Chef's Touches*), and the apples' rounded edges sitting on the caramel. Add as many apple halves as you can fit, so that they hold themselves together, leaving a hole in the centre.

3. Cut the remaining apple halves into quarters and fill up the hole in the centre, placing 2–3 quarters into it vertically and then positioning remaining ones on top, core-side down. Cover the top of the mould tightly with foil to keep the steam in, and bake for 1 hour 30 minutes–1 hour 40 minutes.

Recipe continued overleaf

CHEF'S TOUCHES

The butter and sugar will split to begin with, but as the mixture turns to caramel, they will combine smoothly. *The colour needs to be a light caramel, as it will darken further in the oven.*

If your apples are too large, *you may need to cut them into quarters to build the tart, and as a result the tart may cook a little quicker.*

Using the shape of the apple, *slightly wider at the top and tapered at the bottom, helps you compact your apples tightly as you lay them in the mould.*

The size of apples will affect the cooking time, *as will using different varieties of apple, so if for any reason the apples are still firm, continue cooking until they are cooked and becoming soft.*

4. Prick the apples in the centre with a toothpick or a small knife. They need to be cooked and totally soft (*see Chef's Touches*). Remove the foil and press down the top of the apples with a small palette knife or the back of a spoon to flatten. Carefully holding onto the apples with a large wooden spoon, drain away roughly two-thirds of the cooking juice from the mould. Lay the disc of puff pastry on top of the hot apples, pushing the excess down around the edges of the baked apples to secure them in place.

5. Place back in the oven and bake for about 40 minutes, or until the puff pastry is totally baked. Remove the tart from the oven and leave to rest on the side for a good couple of hours before de-moulding.

SERVING

6. Place the mould/pan on the hob and gently warm it up, while trying to spin by hand the tart and get it loose. Remove from the heat and carefully place the serving plate face down on top of the mould. Using a dry cloth, flip the pan and the plate over and shake the tart out onto the plate. Serve with vanilla ice cream or crème fraîche. Best eaten fresh, though stored in an airtight container it will last for up to 2 days.

strawberry & pistachio tart

serves 6–8

PREPARATION TIME
20 minutes

COOKING TIME
30 minutes

SPECIAL EQUIPMENT
20 cm (8 in) tart ring, 2 cm (¾ in) deep, piping bags, medium plain nozzle and 8 mm (⅜ in) plain nozzle

PLANNING AHEAD
Make the sablé pastry to the point of being ready to roll, pistachio paste and the almond cream; you may have some ready in the freezer from a previous batch.
Toast the pistachios.

INGREDIENTS

For the tart case
250 g (9 oz) sablé pastry (*see page 24*)
Butter, for greasing
70 g (2½ oz) Pistachio Paste (*see page 60*)
150 g (5½ oz) Almond Cream (*see page 56*)

For the soaking syrup
30 g (1 oz) Sugar Syrup (*see page 70*)
10 g (½ oz/2 teaspoons) water
5 g (¼ oz/1 teaspoon) kirsch eau de vie

To decorate
150 g (5½ oz) Pastry Cream (*see page 54*)
20 g (¾ oz) Pistachio Paste (*see page 60*)
300 g (10½ oz) fresh strawberries, washed
30 g (1 oz) strawberry jam
10 g (½ oz) toasted pistachios (*see page 184*), roughly chopped
Icing (powdered) sugar, for dusting

Pistachio and strawberries – what's not to love?!

METHOD

1. Preheat the oven to 170°C fan (340°F).
2. Roll out the sablé pastry to a disc of about 25 cm (10 in) which is 3 mm (⅛ in) thickness. With your fingers, spread a thin coat of soft butter all over the inside the tart ring. Line it with the pastry (*see page 24*). Now trim the edges with a paring knife or by rolling a rolling pin over the top. Place on a baking tray lined with baking parchment and set aside.
3. With a whisk, combine the pistachio paste with the almond cream. Transfer to a piping bag fitted with a medium plain nozzle and pipe it evenly inside the tart case.
4. Bake for about 30 minutes, or until it is nice and golden, checking the base of the tart is cooked by lifting it carefully with a palette knife. Remove from the oven and leave to cool completely.

FINISHING THE TART

5. Meanwhile, in a medium bowl, whisk the pastry cream until smooth and combine with the pistachio paste. Fill a piping bag fitted with a 8 mm (⅜ in) plain nozzle and set aside.
6. In a small jug, combine all the ingredients for the soaking syrup and brush all over the top of the cooled almond and pistachio cream in the tart case. Now pipe the pistachio pastry cream evenly all over the top, leaving a border of up to 2 cm (¾ in) around the edges of the tart. Remove the strawberry stems and slice them all into 1 cm (½ in) slices, then arrange these on top of the tart. Warm the strawberry jam in a small pan over a low heat to loosen, then brush the jam over the top of the strawberries. Sprinkle with the toasted pistachios, and with a small sieve, dust icing sugar generously over the edges of the tart for extra visual impact. Best eaten fresh, though stored in an airtight container it will last for up to 2 days.

custard tart

serves 6

PREPARATION TIME
20 minutes

COOKING TIME
20–22 minutes to blind-bake the tart, plus 40–45 minutes

SPECIAL EQUIPMENT
21 cm (8¼ in) loose-bottomed fluted pie tin, 3.5 cm (1½ in) deep, temperature probe, small grater for the nutmeg

PLANNING AHEAD
Prepare the sablé pastry to the point of being ready to roll, and the egg wash.

INGREDIENTS

For the tart case
300 g (10½ oz) Sablé Pastry
  (*see page 24*)
butter, for greasing
25 g (1 oz) Egg Wash (*see
  page 70*)

For the custard filling
6 egg yolks
1 egg

70 g (2½ oz/⅓ cup) caster
  (superfine) sugar
90 g (3¼ oz/scant ½ cup)
  whole milk
380 g (12½ oz/1⅓ cup)
  whipping cream
¼ nutmeg, for grating
fresh fruit coulis, to serve

CHEF'S TOUCHES

When nearly cooked and you have a trembling custard filling, *you can turn off the oven for a few minutes to avoid overcooking the custard.*

This is another classic British dessert, typically served with grated nutmeg on top. I was not too sure about it to begin with, as I associate nutmeg with savoury baking, especially quiche, but over time this recipe has grown on me. It's best served freshly baked and at room temperature.

METHOD

BLIND-BAKING THE TART CASE
1. Preheat the oven to 180°C fan (350°F).
2. Roll out the sablé pastry to a disc 28 cm (11 in) in diameter and 3 mm (⅛ in) thick. Spread a thin coat of soft butter all over the inside of the tin with your fingers. Line it with the pastry and trim the edges by rolling a rolling pin over the top of the tin. Blind-bake for 20–22 minutes, or until nice and golden. Brush the egg wash all over the inside of the tart case to waterproof it and place back in the oven for a couple of minutes to cook it. Set aside.

MAKING THE CUSTARD
3. Reduce the oven temperature to 140°C fan (280°F).
4. In a medium bowl, whisk together the egg yolks, egg and sugar, then add the milk and cream. In a medium saucepan, warm the mixture gently over a medium heat, using a rubber spatula to stir continuously until it reaches 50°C (122°F). Pour into the tart case and grate the nutmeg over the top.
5. Place the tart carefully on a rack in the middle of the oven and bake for 40–45 minutes, or until the custard is set (*see Chef's Touches*). Remove from the oven and allow to cool completely before carefully removing the tart from the tin. Set aside and ideally enjoy on the same day, served at room temperature with fresh fruit coulis.

pear almondine tarte

serves 6

Also known as tarte Bourdaloue, a reference to the Parisian pastry chef who created the dessert back in the day. For me, this is one of the simple, classic tarts which never fails to please and it is also relatively simple to make.

PREPARATION TIME
20 minutes

COOKING TIME
40–50 minutes

SPECIAL EQUIPMENT
20 cm (8 in) tart ring, piping bag and 6–8 mm (¼–⅜ in) plain nozzle

PLANNING AHEAD
Prepare the sablé pastry to the point of being ready to roll and the almond cream. You can also poach the pears the day before if that helps.

INGREDIENTS

For poaching the pears
500 ml (17 fl oz/generous 2 cups) water
150 g (5½ oz/⅔ cup) caster (superfine) sugar
½ teaspoon lemon juice
2 large, ripe William pears

For the tart
250 g (9 oz) Sablé Pastry (*see page 24*)
300 g (10½ oz) Almond Cream (*see page 56*)
10 g (½ oz) flaked (slivered) almonds
10 g (½ oz/2 teaspoons) icing (powdered) sugar, for dusting

METHOD

POACHING THE PEARS

1. In a medium saucepan, bring the water, sugar and lemon juice to the boil. Meanwhile, peel the pears and cut the top off just one pear, about 3 cm (1¼ in) down from the tip. Cut the rest into quarters and remove the stems and cores with a melon baller or similar. Add the pear quarters and the pear top to the boiling syrup and bring it back to the boil for 10 seconds. Take the pan off the heat and leave the pears to rest in the syrup for 3–5 minutes, or until partially cooked (*see Chef's Touches*). Scoop the pears out of the syrup and drain them in a colander. Transfer to a flat tray lined with a double layer of paper towels to absorb the excess moisture.

MAKING THE TART

2. Preheat the oven to 170°C fan (340°F).
3. Roll out the sablé pastry into a disc about 24 cm (until about 2–3 mm (⅛ in) thick. On a lightly floured surface, line the tart ring with the pastry and trim the edges with a paring knife. Place on a flat baking tray lined with baking parchment. Using a piping bag with a 6–8 mm (¼–⅜ in) plain nozzle, pipe the almond cream evenly all over the tart. Arrange the pear quarters on top in a flower petal pattern, then place the pear top in the middle for a nice rustic finish.
4. Sprinkle the flaked almonds into the gaps and over the almond cream. Bake the tart in the middle of the oven for 40–50 minutes until the pastry is totally baked (*see Chef's Touches*). Remove from the oven and leave to rest on the side for 10–20 minutes to firm up before removing the ring.
5. Prior to serving, sprinkle a little icing sugar around the edges of the tart. If you like, you can also glaze the pears with a little bit of clear fruit jam or jelly.

CHEF'S TOUCHES

The timing for poaching the pears will inevitably vary depending on how ripe they are. *If very ripe, they should cook very quickly. Be careful not to overcook very ripe pears, as they will release far too much juice in the tart when baking later on and make it soggy. On the contrary, if the pears are not ripe enough* or too firm, it will take longer to cook the fruit, so you will need to leave them in the syrup until you can prick a knife into them.

Lift the tart carefully with a palette knife *to see if it is baked underneath.*

flan vanille

serves 6—8

Simply a loose, hot pastry cream in a puff pastry tart case, baked together. One of the first tasks that was given to me as a baker's apprentice when I was fourteen was to bake and sell these on the town's market day. Bakeries in France still sell them, and you could argue that this is our French version of a British custard tart.

PREPARATION TIME
20 minutes

COOKING TIME
50–55 minutes

SPECIAL EQUIPMENT
20 cm (8 in) tart ring, 2.5cm (1 in) deep

PLANNING AHEAD
Prepare the puff pastry.

1. Preheat the oven to 170°C fan (340°F).
2. Roll out the puff pastry until 2 mm (¹⁄₁₆ in) thick. With a sharp knife, cut out a disc about 26 cm (10½ in) in diameter. Line the tin with the pastry and blind-bake with rice or baking beans for about 20 minutes (*see instructions on page 28*). Take out the rice or beans and bake for a further 5 minutes to dry out the inside of the pastry case. When finished, remove from the oven and increase the oven temperature to 180°C fan (350°F).

INGREDIENTS

For the tart case
250 g (9 oz) Quick Puff
  Pastry (*see page 30*),
  or you can also use
  shortcrust if it's easier

For the filling
1 vanilla pod
400 g (14 oz/generous
  1½ cups) whole milk

3 egg yolks
35 g (1¼ oz/¼ cup)
  cornflour (cornstarch)
95 g (3¼ oz/scant ½ cup)
  caster (superfine) sugar
15 g (½ oz) unsalted butter,
  diced
65 g (2¼ oz) crème fraîche

3. Meanwhile, split the vanilla pod in half lengthways and scrape the seeds into a medium saucepan over a medium heat. Add the pod and the milk and bring to the boil. In a bowl, whisk together the egg yolks, cornflour and sugar. As soon as the vanilla milk boils, remove from the heat and pour a quarter over the egg yolk mixture and whisk rapidly. Pour this mixture back into the pan with the milk and whisk. Place back over a medium heat, whisking continuously until the mixture starts thickening. Take the pan off the heat to whisk until smooth. When thickened and smooth, place the pan back on the heat for a quick boil. Take off the heat, remove the vanilla pod with a fork and whisk in the butter and the crème fraîche.
4. Pour the mixture into the blind-baked tart case and bake for about 25 minutes. Leave on the side to cool for 15 minutes before removing the ring. Let the flan cool completely before slicing it (*see Chef's Touches*).

CHEF'S TOUCHES

Once completely cooled, *the flan will be more set firmly and easier to cut. You might even want to leave it in the refrigerator for 1 hour to firm up.*

travel cakes

CHAPTER 5

blueberry muffins

I love making these with wild blueberries, which tend to have more flavour than the regular much larger blueberries you find in the shops.

◆ ◇ ◇

makes 15

PREPARATION TIME
15 minutes

COOKING TIME
30 minutes

SPECIAL EQUIPMENT
12-hole muffin tray (7.5/3 in diameter, 4 cm/1½ in deep) and 15 paper muffin cases

PLANNING AHEAD
On a flat tray lined with baking parchment, bake a bit of crumble mixture at 170°C fan (340°F) for about 6 minutes. Break into small pieces and sprinkle on top of the muffins before baking them for added texture.

INGREDIENTS

240 g (8½ oz/scant 2 cups) plain (all-purpose) flour
9 g (¼ oz) baking powder
80 g (2¾ oz) unsalted butter, at room temperature
15 g (½ oz/1 tablespoon) grapeseed oil, or any neutral flavour oil
small pinch of salt
zest of ¼ lemon
165 g (5¾ oz/¾ cup) caster (superfine) sugar

4 eggs, beaten
3 g (½ teaspoon) vanilla extract
195 g (7 oz) fresh blueberries or wild blueberries (*see Chef's Touches*)
40 g (1½ oz) part-baked crumble, *optional* (*see page 230 – replace the cocoa powder for plain flour*), for topping
icing (powdered) sugar, for dusting

CHEF'S TOUCHES

You can switch *the blueberries for whole blackcurrants for a slightly stronger kick of flavours in the muffin.*

METHOD

1. Preheat the oven to 170°C fan (340°F).
2. In a medium bowl, siift the flour and baking powder together. In a separate large bowl, whisk together the butter, oil, salt, lemon zest and sugar.
3. Add the beaten eggs, followed gradually by the vanilla extract, mixing between the additions, then add the sifted flour mixture. When smooth, add the blueberries and fold in quickly. Transfer 50–60 g (1¾–2 oz) of the batter into each muffin mould lined with a paper case. The batter makes 15 muffins, so you'll need to work in batches unless you have two muffin trays.
4. Cover each muffin with a little bit of crumble, if using. Bake for 25–30 minutes. Remove from the oven, then cool for 5 minutes before removing from the moulds, dusting with some icing sugar and serving. Stored in an airtight container, these will last for up to 2 days.

muscovado & dark rum fruit cake

makes 1 loaf cake

PREPARATION TIME
10 minutes

COOKING TIME
55 minutes

SPECIAL EQUIPMENT
25 x 8 cm (10 x 3¼ in) loaf tin (pan), 8 cm (3¼ in) deep, lined with silicone baking parchment, mixer with paddle attachment

PLANNING AHEAD
Marinate the fruit for at least 2 hours the night before.

INGREDIENTS

For the fruit
50 g (1¾ oz/scant ½ cup) sultanas (golden raisins)
50 g (1¾ oz/¼ cup) mixed peel
40 g (1½ oz/¼ cup) dried figs, roughly chopped
50 g (1¾ oz) dried cranberries
60 g (2 oz/¼ cup) dark rum

For the cake
50 g (1¾ oz/scant ½ cup) icing (powdered) sugar
185 g (6½ oz/1½ cups) plain (all-purpose) flour
8 g (¼ oz) baking powder

120 g (4¼ oz) unsalted butter, at room temperature
30 g (1 oz/2 tablespoons) sunflower oil
100 g (3½ oz/½ cup) muscovado sugar or light brown sugar
zest of 1 lemon
3 whole eggs, beaten (150 g/5½ oz)
70 g (2½ oz/⅓ cup) whole glacé cherries
10 ml (2 teaspoons) dark rum, for brushing
20 g (¾ oz) warm apricot jam (*optional*)

I have had to try several versions of this to find the one that I love. I hope you will enjoy it too.

METHOD

PREPARING THE FRUIT
1. Combine all the fruits in a container with the dark rum and cover with a lid. Heat in the microwave for 3 minutes, then set aside in the refrigerator overnight.

MAKING THE CAKE
2. Preheat the oven to 180°C fan (350°F) and line the cake tin with silicone baking parchment (*see Chef's Touches*).
3. In a bowl, sift the icing sugar, flour and baking powder together. In the mixer using the paddle attachment, combine the butter, oil, muscovado sugar and lemon zest on a low speed. Gradually add the beaten eggs, followed by the sifted flour mixture. Fold in the macerated fruits (*see Chef's Touches*). Pour into the prepared tin and level the mixture with a rubber spatula. Randomly push in the glacé cherries, ensuring they are completely covered.

BAKING
4. Bake for about 40 minutes, then reduce the oven temperature to 165°C fan (330°F) and bake for a further 15 minutes. To check if it is cooked through, insert a small knife into the middle of the cake; if it comes out clean, the cake is done. Remove from the oven, then brush the top of the cake with the dark rum. Remove the cake from the tin using the parchment 'handles' and leave to cool completely on a rack.
5. For a shiny finish, brush the top of the cake with warm apricot jam. Stored in an airtight container, this will last for up to 3 days.

Line the cake tin *with a band of baking parchment the same length as the tin, overlapping it by a couple of centimetres (¾ inch) on each side. Fold and pinch the parchment around the rim of the cake tin to create two handles that you will use to pull the cake out of the tin when baked.*

When in the tin, before baking, *pipe a thin line of soft butter along the centre to help with the cracking of the cake.*

For a bit of decoration *to make it extra-special, add 100 g (3½ oz) glacé cherries on top.*

You can toss the fruits *in a bit of plain (all-purpose) flour before adding them to the mixture for them not to sink too much down to bottom of the mould when baking.*

double chocolate & vanilla marble cake

makes 1 loaf

This recipe is inspired by one I used to make when working at The Ritz in Paris. On this occasion, I have made it even more chocolatey by glazing it with dark chocolate for extra flavour and extra texture.

PREPARATION TIME
15 minutes

COOKING TIME
45–50 minutes

SPECIAL EQUIPMENT
Mixer with paddle attachment, 25 x 8 cm (10 x 3¼ in) loaf tin, 8 cm (3¼ in) deep 2 piping bags with 2 large plain 1 cm (½ in) nozzles, small jug, temperature probe

INGREDIENTS

200 g (7 oz) unsalted butter, at room temperature, plus (*optional*) extra for greasing

200 g (7 oz/generous ¾ cup) caster (superfine) sugar

4 eggs, beaten

½ teaspoon vanilla extract

240 g (8½ oz/scant 2 cups) plain (all-purpose) flour

7 g (¼ oz) baking powder

25 g (1 oz/scant 2 tablespoons) whipping cream

15 g (1 tablespoon) cocoa powder

25 ml (scant 2 tablespoons) hot water

For the chocolate glaze (optional)

200 g (7 oz) 60–70% good-quality dark chocolate

30 g (1 oz/2 tablespoons) sunflower oil, plus (*optional*) extra for greasing

CHEF'S TOUCHES

Line the cake tin *with a band of baking parchment the same length as the tin, overlapping it by a couple of centimetres (¾ inch) on each side. Fold and pinch the parchment around the rim of the cake tin to create two handles that you will use to pull the cake out of the tin when baked.*

METHOD

MAKING THE CAKE

1. Preheat the oven to 175°C fan (345°F). Lightly brush the cake tin with a thin coating of melted butter or oil and line it with silicone baking parchment (*see Chef's Touches*).

2. In the mixer with the paddle attachment, cream together the butter and sugar until light and fluffy, then gradually add the beaten eggs and the vanilla extract. In a bowl, sift together the flour and baking powder, then add to the butter mixture on a low speed. When fully combined, add the whipping cream.

3. In a separate bowl, whisk together the cocoa powder and hot water until smooth. Add about 300 g (10½ oz) of the cake mixture and stir. Using two piping bags, both with a 1 cm (½ in) plain nozzle, alternate piping bands of both the light and dark mixture lengthways into the tin. Marble the cake by passing and weaving a small knife or palette knife through the middle of the batter, twice.

4. Bake for about 50 minutes. Prick the centre of the cake with a small wooden toothpick or a small knife; if it comes out clean, the cake is baked. Remove from the oven and lift the cake out of the tin using the parchment 'handles' on a cooling rack. You can now eat it as it is or glaze it when completely cool.

GLAZING

5. Melt the chocolate in a small jug over a warm water bain-marie or slowly in the microwave to reach a temperature of 40°C (104°F) maximum. Using a rubber spatula, mix in the sunflower oil.

6. Cover a small tray with cling film (plastic wrap) or baking parchment and place the cooling rack with the cooled marble cake on top of it. Gradually pour the warm chocolate glaze all over the cake, moving the jug in a tight zigzag from one side to the other. Place the cake in the refrigerator to set for 30 minutes.

7. With a slightly warm blade, carefully scrape and loosen the cake from the cooling rack and transfer it onto a nice serving plate. Keep at room temperature in a cool area in your kitchen for up to 3 days.

madeleines

18–20 madeleines (*see Chef's Touches*)

A very French little afternoon tea cake with a typical seashell look, a buttery flavour and a fluffy texture. For me, there is definitely a feel-good factor when you achieve the perfect little hump on top, and when you eat these beautiful cakes slightly warm! Why not enjoy with a bit of chocolate sauce?

PREPARATION TIME
15 minutes, plus at least 2 hours resting

COOKING TIME
6–8 minutes

SPECIAL EQUIPMENT
Non-stick madeleine tray, piping bag (1 cm/½ in plain nozzle)

PLANNING AHEAD
Prep the madeleine mixture at least 2 hours before baking.

INGREDIENTS

For the moulds
30 g (1 oz/¼ cup) unsalted butter, softened
30 g (1 oz/¼ cup) plain (all-purpose) flour

For the batter
115 g (4 oz/scant 1 cup) plain (all-purpose) flour
5 g (1 teaspoon) baking powder
zest of ½ lemon
80 g (2¾ oz/⅔ cup) caster (superfine) sugar

2 eggs, beaten
2 g (½ teaspoon) salt
2 g (½ teaspoon) vanilla extract
5 g (1 teaspoon) honey
80 g (2¾ oz) unsalted butter, melted

warm chocolate sauce (*see page 60*), to serve (*optional*)

METHOD

PREPARING THE MOULDS

1. Thinly brush the butter evenly inside the moulds. Cover all over with the flour and tap away the excess. Set aside in the refrigerator to set until needed.

MAKING THE MADELEINES

2. In a bowl, sift together the flour and baking powder and set aside. In another bowl, mix the lemon zest with the sugar, then add the beaten eggs and salt and whisk. Add the vanilla extract and honey, followed by the sifted flour mixture. Gradually add the lukewarm melted butter and combine until smooth.

3. Cover the mixture with cling film (plastic wrap) and leave to cool and firm up in the refrigerator for at least a couple of hours.

BAKING

4. Preheat the oven to 180°C fan (350°F) with a baking stone or heavy baking tray inside.

5. Using a piping bag and a 1 cm (½ in) plain nozzle, pipe the madeleine mixture into the mould cavities, filling each one three-quarters full Place the moulds on the hot tray or stone and bake for 6–8 minutes until nice and golden, depending on the strength of your oven. Remove from the oven and, with a small pointy knife, tilt the madeleines quickly on their side to cool down and firm up. Best eaten just warm … but they will keep for up to 3 days stored in an airtight container.

CHEF'S TOUCHES

For a nice top on your madeleines, *make sure you create a thermal shock when baking, by piping your very cold mixture into a very cold mould, then placing the mould onto a hot tray in the oven should do the trick.*

Also, you can pipe a little point of soft butter *exactly where you want the dome/pompom to rise on top of the madeleines.*

raspberry financiers

makes 12

PREPARATION TIME
15 minutes

COOKING TIME
10–12 minutes

SPECIAL EQUIPMENT
12-hole non-stick muffin tray (moulds 6–7 cm/2½–2¾ in in diameter x 3–4cm/1¼–1½ in deep), piping bag with a plain nozzle (1 cm/½ in diameter)

PLANNING AHEAD
Before weighing out your ingredients for the recipe, place a medium baking tray, about 20 cm (8 in) square, in the freezer to stop the cooking of the butter when the time comes.

Financiers are the reason I became a pastry chef. I remember being six or seven years old and shopping with my aunt back in France and, because I behaved while shopping with her, she took me to a pastry shop, where I discovered this beautiful cake. I found myself emotionally affected by its flavour and texture, and hoped to be able to eat more at my leisure. This train of thoughts eventually grew into a pastry chef career for me and, of course, a similar version of this beautiful cake now features in my kitchen as part of our little coffee treats. The recipe below is made with raspberries, but you can also make them plain.

INGREDIENTS

110 g (3¾ oz) unsalted butter, plus extra for greasing
75 g (2½ oz/⅔ cup) ground almonds
40 g (1½ oz/scant 3 tablespoons) caster (superfine) sugar
125 g (4½ oz/1 cup) icing (powdered) sugar, sifted

50 g (1¾ oz/scant ½ cup) plain (all-purpose) flour
135 g (4¾ oz) egg whites
pinch of salt
½ teaspoon vanilla extract
dash of dark rum
12 large raspberries

METHOD

1. Preheat the oven to 190°C fan (375°F). and lightly grease the holes of the muffin tray with butter

2. In a small pan, melt the butter over a medium heat until it starts foaming and the foam is light brown in colour (*see Chef's Touches*). Transfer it immediately into the cold tray to stop the butter from cooking further and cool it down. Set aside.

3. In a medium bowl, whisk together the ground almonds, caster sugar, icing sugar and flour. In a separate medium bowl, working by hand, whisk the egg whites with the salt until you have soft peaks. Fold in the flour mixture. Whisk in the cooled butter, then add the vanilla extract and rum.

4. Fill a piping bag with the mixture and pipe into the prepared muffin tray, filling each mould up to one-third of the way up the sides. Place a whole raspberry on top of each one.

5. Bake for 10–12 minutes, or until nice and golden. Remove from the oven, de-mould straight away and place on a wire rack to cool for about 15 minutes. Enjoy fresh, but stored in an airtight container they will keep for up to 3 days.

CHEF'S TOUCHES

This stage is called noisette or hazelnut butter, *as it develops a nutty smell and taste and a golden-brown colour. Cooking the butter further or letting it become dark at*

the bottom of the pan would create bitterness, and it will not smell and taste nutty as it should.

You can also bake a large financier *in a 20 cm (8 in) ring using 250–300 g (9–10½ oz) mixture. This makes a fantastic base for a tart.*

scones

makes 15

A traditional scone studded with moist golden sultanas. This dilemma has gone on for a very long time in England: which way will you eat yours, jam or cream on top?

PREPARATION TIME
20 minutes, plus 40 minutes proving

COOKING TIME
15–18 minutes

SPECIAL EQUIPMENT
Plain cutter (5.5 cm/2¼ in diameter)

PLANNING AHEAD
Get the cream and jam ready.

INGREDIENTS

500 g (1 lb 2 oz/4 cups) plain (all-purpose) flour, plus extra for dusting
pinch of salt
35 g (1¼ oz) baking powder
75 g (2½ oz) unsalted butter at room temperature
100 g (3½ oz/scant ½ cup) caster (superfine) sugar

150 g (5½ oz/1¼ cups) sultanas (golden raisins)
2 eggs, plus 1, beaten, for egg wash
160 g (5¾ oz/⅔ cup) whole milk
clotted cream and strawberry jam, to serve

METHOD

1. In a large bowl, sift together the flour, salt and baking powder, twice. By hand, rub in the butter to form a breadcrumb-like texture, then add the sugar and golden sultanas.
2. In a jug, whisk together the eggs and the milk, then add this to the flour. Transfer the mixture to the table and continue to knead into a dough for 5–10 minutes, or until smooth.
3. Dust the surface with flour and roll out the dough to about 2.5 cm (1 in) thick with the rough side on top. Leave the dough to relax a little for a minute before cutting. Using the plain cutter, cut out the scones, dipping the cutter into flour between uses and pressing and levelling the dough in the cutter by hand. Turn the scones out upside down onto a flat tray lined with silicone baking parchment. The smooth side should be now on the top.
4. Lightly brush the top of the scones with the beaten egg and rest for at least 20 minutes in a warm cupboard or near the oven.
5. Preheat the oven to 170°C fan (340°F).
6. Brush the scones with the egg wash again and leave to prove and dry out for another 20 minutes.
7. Bake for about 15–18 minutes until nice and golden. Remove from the oven and leave to cool until warm. Serve with clotted cream and jam, in whichever order you like! Stored in an airtight container, these will keep for up to 3 days. Simply warm up in the oven before eating.

chocolate scones

makes 15

PREPARATION TIME
20 minutes, plus 40 minutes proving

COOKING TIME
15–18 minutes

SPECIAL EQUIPMENT
Plain cutter (5.5 cm/2¼ in diameter), probe thermometer

PLANNING AHEAD
Get the cream and jam ready.

INGREDIENTS

500 g (1 lb 2 oz/4 cups) plain (all-purpose) flour, plus extra for dusting

1 g salt

35 g (1¼ oz) baking powder

170 g (6 oz/¾ cup) whole milk, cold

50 g (1¾ oz) 70% chocolate, melted to 40°C (104°F)

75 g (2½ oz) unsalted butter, at room temperature

100 g (3½ oz/scant ½ cup) caster (superfine) sugar

2 eggs, plus 1, beaten, for egg wash

100 g (3½ oz) 70% dark chocolate, chopped into small pieces

clotted cream and sour cherry jam or marmalade, to serve

I developed this recipe for a well-known French chocolate company, and I love it served with a good sour cherry jam.

METHOD

1. Preheat the oven to 170°C fan (340°F).

2. In a large bowl, sift together the flour, salt and baking powder, twice. In a small saucepan over a low heat, warm the milk to 50°C (122°F), then take off the heat and gradually whisk in the melted chocolate. Beat the 2 eggs and add them to this mixture. By hand, rub the butter into the flour mixture to form a breadcrumb-like texture, then combine with the egg and chocolate mixture to form a dough.

3. Knead the dough for 5–10 minutes, or until smooth. Dust the surface with flour and roll out the dough to about to 2.5 cm (1 in) thick with the rough side on top. Leave the dough to relax a little before cutting. Using the plain cutter, cut out the scones, dipping the cutter into flour between uses, pressing and levelling the dough by hand in the cutter. Turn out the scones upside down onto a flat tray lined with silicone baking parchment.

4. The smooth side should now be on the top. Lightly brush the top of the scones with the remaining beaten egg, then rest for at least 20 minutes in a warm cupboard or near the oven. Brush the scones with the egg wash again and leave to prove and dry out for another 20 minutes.

5. Bake for about 15–18 minutes until nice and golden. Serve with clotted cream and sour cherry jam or marmalade. Stored in an airtight container, these will keep for up to 3 days. Simply warm up in the oven before eating.

banana & rum cake

1 loaf

PREPARATION TIME
15 minutes

COOKING TIME
1 hour

SPECIAL EQUIPMENT
25 x 8 cm (10 x 3¼ in) loaf tin (pan), 8 cm (3¼ in) deep, mixer with paddle attachment or food processor

PLANNING AHEAD
You can collect and freeze any overripe bananas (leave the skins on). They will go black. When you have enough, defrost them for a couple of hours for best results and remove the skins.

You can make this cake when you have collected some overripe bananas. It's very important for the cake to develop a great banana flavour, so the bananas need to be really, really, really overripe!

(see Chef's Touches)

INGREDIENTS

100 g (3½ oz) unsalted butter
200 g (7 oz/generous ¾ cup) caster (superfine) sugar
2 eggs (about 110 g/3¾ oz)
300 g (10½ oz) very ripe bananas
200 g (7 oz/1⅓ cups) plain (all-purpose) flour
3 g (½ teaspoon) baking powder
7 g (1½ teaspoons) bicarbonate of soda (baking soda)
75 g (2½ oz/5 tablespoons) cold water
20 ml (1½ tablespoons) dark rum

For the lime rum glaze (*optional*)
125 g (4½ oz) warm apricot jelly, melted
25 g (1 oz/scant 2 tablespoons) dark rum
zest of ½ lime
25 g (1 oz/scant 2 tablespoons) lime juice
250 g (9 oz/2 cups) icing (powdered) sugar

METHOD

MAKING THE CAKE

1. Preheat the oven to 165°C fan (330°F) and line the loaf tin with silicone baking parchment (*see Chef's Touches*).
2. Using a mixer with a paddle attachment (or a food processor), cream together the butter and sugar on a low speed for 3 minutes, then gradually add the eggs, followed by the peeled and mashed bananas. In a bowl, sift together the flour and baking powder, then add to the banana mixture.
3. Dissolve the bicarbonate in the cold water and rum and gradually add to the batter. Pour the mixture into the prepared tin and bake for about 1 hour. Remove from the tin using the parchment 'handles' and leave to cool on a wire rack. You can enjoy the cake as it is, or for extra flavour, apply the glaze below.

GLAZING

4. Remove the baking parchment from the loaf and place the cake on a baking tray set on top of the cooling rack.
5. Lightly brush the cake all over with the warm melted apricot jelly.
6. In a small saucepan, gently warm the rum, lime zest and juice, and icing sugar to form a warm (40–50°C) white, cloudy glaze. Brush this all over the cake on top of the apricot jelly and leave for a few minutes to set.
7. Preheat the oven to 190°C fan (375°F). Place the glazed cake in the oven and turn the oven off. Leave the cake inside until the glaze becomes slightly transparent: 3–4 minutes maximum. Remove from the oven and leave to cool completely. Stored in an airtight container, this will keep for up to 3 days.

CHEF'S TOUCHES

Line the cake tin *with a band of baking parchment the same length as the tin, overlapping it by a couple of centimetres (¾ inch) on each side. Fold and pinch the parchment around the* rim of the cake tin to create two handles that you will use to pull the cake out of the tin when baked.

my gluten-free lemon drizzle cake

The lemon cake has always been part of our welcome at Le Manoir aux Quat'Saisons, and its recipe has constantly evolved to make it lighter and more flavoursome every time. It's now made even lighter by using gluten-free self-raising flour. You will need 5–6 lemons for this recipe, depending on their size.

◆ ◇ ◇

makes 1 loaf

PREPARATION TIME
10 minutes, plus 1 hour resting

COOKING TIME
45 minutes

SPECIAL EQUIPMENT
25 x 7 cm (10 x 3 in) loaf tin, 8 cm (3¼ in) deep, pastry brush

PLANNING AHEAD
The zest and the juice of about 5–6 lemons can be prepared a bit in advance. You can also make the soaking syrup and glaze ahead of time.

INGREDIENTS

For the soaking syrup
80 g (2¾ oz/5 tablespoons) lemon juice
30 g (1 oz/2 tablespoons) water
40 g (1½ oz/scant 3 tablespoons) caster (superfine) sugar

For the cake batter
3 medium eggs (160 g/5¾ oz)
200 g (7 oz/generous ¾ cup) caster (superfine) sugar
approx. 13 g (½ oz) finely grated lemon zest
95 g (3¼ oz/scant ½ cup) double (heavy) cream
135 g (4¾ oz/generous 1 cup) gluten-free self-raising flour (see Chef's Touches)

70 g (2½ oz/½ cup) potato flour
6 g (¼ oz) baking powder
15 ml (1 tablespoon) dark rum
small pinch of salt
45 g (1½ oz/3 tablespoons) olive oil, plus extra for greasing

For the glaze
80 g (2¾ oz) apricot jelly
1 tablespoon water
approx. 3 g (1 teaspoon) finely grated lemon zest
30 g (2 tablespoons) lemon juice
165 g (6oz) icing (powdered) sugar

METHOD

MAKING THE SOAKING SYRUP

1. In a small saucepan, bring all the ingredients to a quick boil, then set aside to cool.

FOR THE CAKE

2. In a large bowl, whisk together the eggs, sugar, lemon zest and double cream. In a medium bowl, sift together the self-raising flour, potato flour and baking powder. Add to the egg mixture and whisk together, then add the rum, salt and olive oil. Combine until smooth and rest, covered, in the refrigerator for at least 1 hour.

3. Meanwhile, brush the inside of the loaf tin with a thin coating of olive oil and line it with baking parchment (see Chef's Touches).

4. Preheat the oven to 170°C fan (340°F). Fill the prepared tin with the cake batter and bake on the middle shelf for about 25 minutes. Rotate the tin and bake for a further 20 minutes (see Chef's Touches). De-mould the cake by pulling on the parchment 'handles' and transfer it onto a cooling rack sitting over a baking tray. Peel off the baking parchment from the sides of the cake and brush it all over with the soaking syrup while still hot. Leave to cool and firm up for at least 30 minutes.

GLAZING THE CAKE

5. Preheat the oven to 190°C fan (375°F). Remove the remaining parchment from the cake and place the cake back on the rack with the tray underneath.

6. In a small saucepan, bring the apricot jelly and the water to a quick boil, then lightly brush it over the cake.

7. In a separate small saucepan, gently warm the lemon zest, juice and icing sugar to about 60°C (140°F), stirring continuously to form a loose cloudy glaze. Brush this glaze all over the cake and leave to set for a few minutes. Turn the oven off and place the cake inside until the glaze becomes slightly transparent – 3–4 minutes maximum. Remove from the oven and let cool completely. Release the cake from the rack with a palette knife before serving. Stored in an airtight container it will last for up to 3 days.

Line the cake tin *with a band of baking parchment the same length as the tin, overlapping it by 2 cm (¾ inch) on each side. Fold and pinch the parchment over the tin's rim to create two handles to pull the cake out.*

You can use also regular self-raising flour *if that is all you have, but using a gluten-free version makes the cake feel lighter.*

To check if the cake is baked, *insert a small knife into the middle of the cake. If it comes out clean, it is done.*

yoghurt cake

serves 6–8

Possibly the first ever cake recipe I made as a kid: straightforward and easy to do, yet delicious. This recipe is done without using a scale, instead using the yoghurt pot to measure the ingredients.

PREPARATION TIME
10 minutes

COOKING TIME
30–32 minutes

SPECIAL EQUIPMENT
20 cm (8 in) fluted loose-bottomed non-stick cake tin (or a plain one will do), pastry brush

PLANNING AHEAD
Keep the yoghurt pot for measuring.

INGREDIENTS

125 g (4½ oz/1 pot) plain yoghurt

2 pots caster (superfine) sugar

Zest of ½ lemon

2 medium eggs

½ pot grapeseed oil, plus extra for greasing

3 pots plain (all-purpose) flour (or self-raising flour without the baking powder below)

¾ teaspoon baking powder

jam or berry compote, to serve (*optional*)

10–20 g (½–1 oz) icing sugar, to serve (*optional*)

CHEF'S TOUCHES

You can also serve *this sponge in a similar way to the Summer Berry Victoria Sponge (see page 172).*

METHOD

1. Preheat the oven to 180°C fan (350°F).
2. In a large bowl, empty the yoghurt out of the pot. Add the sugar, lemon zest and eggs, and whisk together. Add the oil, then the flour and baking powder. Whisk well until completely smooth.
3. Slightly oil the cake tin with a brush. Pour the mixture in and bake in the middle of the oven for 30–32 minutes until nice and golden. Prick the centre of the sponge with a knife; if it comes out clean, the cake should be ready.
4. Take the cake out of the tin and dust lightly with the icing sugar, if using. This is lovely served with jam or a berry compôte on the side. Stored in an airtight container, this will last for up to 3 days.

desserts

CHAPTER 6

summer berry victoria sponge

A British classic loved for its simplicity and texture – but forgive me, my good friends, I'm serving it differently, with plenty of lovely summer berries. Don't worry, it's still simple to make and is a lovely dessert.

serves 6–8

PREPARATION TIME
15 minutes

PLANNING AHEAD
On the day, bake a Victoria sponge and allow it to cool.

INGREDIENTS

1 Victoria Sponge
  (*see page 53*)
Chantilly Cream (*see page 59*), to serve

For the soaking syrup
50 g (1¾ oz) good-quality strawberry jam
20 g (1¾ oz/
  1½ tablespoons) water

To decorate
200 g (7 oz) fresh strawberries

100 g (3½ oz) fresh raspberries
50 g (1¾ oz) fresh blueberries or blackberries (when in season)
2–3 bunches of redcurrants, dipped in caster (superfine) sugar (*optional*)
80 g (2¾ oz) good-quality strawberry or redcurrant jam
icing (powdered) sugar, for dusting

METHOD

1. De-mould and place the baked Victoria sponge upside down on a serving dish.

MAKING THE SOAKING SYRUP

2. In a small pan, bring the water and jam to a quick boil and, with a tablespoon, spread it all over the top of the sponge to soak in, leaving a 2 cm (¾ in) border around the edge.

DECORATING

3. Wash all the fruits separately and rapidly in a bowl of cold water and allow them to drain, then transfer them to a tray lined with a double layer of kitchen paper or a clean tea towel.

4. Hull the strawberries, except for two; keep these whole with the stems on to decorate the dessert. Slice about 10 strawberries into small discs and place all around the edge of the sponge. Cut the rest into quarters and place them in a large bowl with the jam and the raspberries and blueberries. Fold together with a dessertspoon without crushing the fruit. Arrange them harmoniously all over the top of the sponge. Cut the reserved whole strawberries in half vertically, keeping the stems on, and place them on top, along with 2 or 3 nice little bunches of redcurrants. Dust the edges of the sponge generously with icing sugar. Serve with Chantilly cream. Stored in an airtight container, this will keep for up to 2 days.

crêpes suzette

A real French dessert, packed with orange flavours, which smells absolutely incredible. Add a little Grand Marnier *flambage* (flambé in English) at the end; it never fails to impress your guests.

serves 4 (makes 8)

PREPARATION TIME
10 minutes

COOKING TIME
15 minutes

SPECIAL EQUIPMENT
Good-quality large non-stick frying pan

PLANNING AHEAD
The crêpes can be cooked a few hours in advance and set aside until you are ready to finish the dish.

(see page 52)

INGREDIENTS

8 French Crêpes
  (*see page 52*)
30 ml (2 tablespoons) Grand
  Marnier, to flambé
  (*optional*)
vanilla ice cream, to serve
  (*optional*)

**For the orange
and butter sauce**
zest of 1 orange
juice of 4–5 large oranges
  (350–400 ml/12–14 fl oz)
2 large oranges, for
  segments
100 g (3½ oz/scant 1 cup)
  caster (superfine) sugar
25 g (1 oz) unsalted butter
25 ml (scant 2 tablespoons)
  Grand Marnier

CHEF'S TOUCHES

You can serve your crêpes *with a scoop of vanilla ice cream for added freshness and a contrast of temperature.*

METHOD

MAKING THE SAUCE
1. Add the orange zest to the orange juice. Separate the remaining oranges into segments and set aside.
2. Heat a hot large frying pan over a medium heat. Sprinkle over the caster sugar and cook, stirring with a wooden spoon when it starts melting, until it gradually turns into a light golden-brown caramel. Stir in the butter, then the orange zest and juice. Bring the sauce gently to the boil for a couple of minutes to thicken it a little. Add the orange segments and leave them to simmer for 1 minute. Take off the heat and add the Grand Marnier. Set aside.

SERVING
3. When you're ready to serve, bring the sauce to a simmer in a frying pan. Fold each crêpe into quarters and place them in the hot orange butter to warm up. Carefully transfer the crêpes to a serving dish of your choice and arrange them elegantly. Pour over the hot cooking liquor and top with the orange segments.
4. At this point, to flambé, you can warm up the Grand Marnier in a saucepan, light it safely with a long match or lighter, and pour it over the crêpes in front of your guests. Serve with vanilla ice cream.

vanilla crème caramel

When I was working at the Ritz Hotel in Paris, a large version of this French classic had to be available all year round on the dessert trolley.

◆◇◇ ─────────────

makes 5

PREPARATION TIME
20 minutes, plus 2–3 hours cooling

COOKING TIME
50 minutes

SPECIAL EQUIPMENT
5 ramekins or 8–9 cm (3¼–3½ in) flat-based teacups 5 cm (2 in) deep, deep 22 cm (8½ in) square baking tray

PLANNING AHEAD
You can keep the crème caramel in the ramekins for a couple of days in the refrigerator, ready for when you need them.

────────────────── INGREDIENTS ──────────────────

For the caramel
75 g (2½ oz/5 tablespoons) cold water
250 g (9 oz/generous 1 cup) caster (superfine) sugar

110 g (3¾ oz/½ cup) caster (superfine) sugar
1 vanilla pod (bean), halved and scraped
4 eggs
2 egg yolks

For the crème mixture
750 g (1 lb 10 oz/3 cups) whole milk

Palmier biscuits, to serve (optional), *see page 86*

────────────────── CHEF'S TOUCHES ──────────────────

The foil *prevents the ramekins from sliding around too much.*

Stop cooking the caramel before it starts smoking, *as otherwise it will become very dark and very bitter.*

When cooked, *the crème caramel should be wobbly and set, like a drum when you tap gently on top with your finger.*

────────────────── METHOD ──────────────────

PREPARING THE RAMEKINS

1. Line a deep baking tray large enough to fit all the ramekins with a sheet of foil (*see Chef's Touches*). Place the ramekins inside.

2. Pour the water into a medium saucepan, then add the sugar. Over a medium heat, bring it to the boil to dissolve the sugar, then increase the heat to high and cook for 4–5 minutes, or until it turns into a rich brown caramel (*see Chef's Touches*). Quickly pour and divide the caramel evenly between the ramekins, with enough to fully cover the bottom of each mould. Leave on the side to set.

MAKING THE CRÈME CARAMEL

3. Preheat the oven to 150°C fan (300°F).

4. Pour half the milk into a medium saucepan, then add the milk, the sugar and the vanilla pod and bring to the boil. Remove from the heat and allow the milk to infuse for 10–15 minutes.

5. In a medium bowl, whisk together the eggs and yolks, gradually adding the remaining milk. Whisk in the vanilla-infused milk. Remove the vanilla with a fork. Transfer the mixture into a jug and use this to fill the ramekins up to 4 cm (1½ in) deep, or evenly dividing the mixture between the moulds.

6. Pour some hot water into one corner of the baking tray so that it surrounds all the ramekins and reaches the same height as the mixture inside. Place the tray carefully in the oven and cook for 45–50 minutes (*see Chef's Touches*). Carefully remove the tray from the oven and, using a cloth, take each dish out of the hot water and transfer to a cooling rack to cool completely. Transfer to the refrigerator for a couple of hours when completely cold.

TO SERVE

7. To release the crème caramels from the ramekins, press the blade of a paring knife against the inside of each mould and take it around in a full circle, then turn each mould upside down on a serving plate. You could also serve them in the moulds in which they have been cooked. Serve with palmier biscuits, if you like.

coffee & orange crème brûlée

Usually scented with vanilla, this is a crème brûlée with a twist, as it uses orange and coffee for extra depth of flavour. You still have the option to make it vanilla, of course.

serves 5

PREPARATION TIME
10 minutes, plus 30 minutes to infuse the milk

COOKING TIME
20–25 minutes

SPECIAL EQUIPMENT
5 x 11 cm (4¼ in) round dishes, 3–3.5 cm (1¼ in) deep, blowtorch

PREPARING THE COFFEE INFUSION

1. Preheat the oven to 150°C non-fan (300°F). Roast the coffee beans for 7–8 minutes.
2. Meanwhile, in a medium saucepan, bring the cream and the milk to the boil, then take off the heat. Wash the orange and, with a potato peeler, peel large bands of zest from around two-thirds of the fruit and add them to the hot cream and milk. Whisk in the hot toasted coffee beans and leave to infuse, covered, for about 30 minutes. Pass through a sieve and measure out 650 g (1 lb 7 oz) of the infusion (*see Chef's Touches*).

MAKING THE CRÈME MIXTURE

3. In a medium bowl, whisk together the egg yolks, egg and sugar, then add the milk and cream infusion. Pass through a sieve and pour into a jug.
4. Place the dishes in a large, deep, flat baking tray lined with foil. Fill each three-quarters of the way up with the crème brûlée mixture. Carefully pour hot water into one corner of the baking tray to surround all the dishes, adding enough to reach the same height as the mixture inside. Place the tray carefully in the oven.
5. Bake for 20–25 minutes, or until the mixture sets but is still just trembling in the middle. Carefully remove the tray from the oven and, using a cloth, take each dish out of the hot water, placing them on a cooling rack to cool completely.

TO SERVE

6. Sprinkle with a thin coating of demerara sugar and caramelise the tops with a blowtorch. It's always nice to eat a crème brûlée with some lovely shortbread or biscuits. I'll leave that up to you...

INGREDIENTS

For the coffee infusion
75 g (2½ oz) coffee beans
350 g (12 oz) whipping cream
450 g (1 lb/generous 1¾ cups) whole milk
1 orange

For the crème mixture
7 egg yolks
1 egg
110 g (3¾ oz/½ cup) caster (superfine) sugar
demerara sugar, for sprinkling

Shortbread or biscuits, to serve (*optional*)

CHEF'S TOUCHES

For vanilla crème brûlée, *combine 325 g (11 oz/1⅓ cups) each of cold whole milk and cold whipping cream with the seeds from 1 vanilla pod, then pick up the method above at step 3.*

The coffee beans will absorb some of the cream and milk, so some weight will be lost. You will therefore need to replace it to keep a very creamy texture once baked.

waffles

makes 10–14

PREPARATION TIME
10 minutes, plus 1–1½ hours resting

COOKING TIME
2½ minutes per waffle

SPECIAL EQUIPMENT
Good-quality traditional or electric waffle iron, one-cal oil spray or a small spray bottle

PLANNING AHEAD
Make the batter 1 hour before cooking the waffles and prepare any garnishes you would like to eat them with.

INGREDIENTS

250 g (9 oz/2 cups) plain (all-purpose) flour
pinch of salt
7 g (¼ oz) baking powder
3 egg yolks
40 g (1½ oz/scant 3 tablespoons) caster (superfine) sugar
2 g (½ teaspoon) vanilla extract (*optional*)
195 g (6 ¾ oz/scant 1 cup) full-fat milk, lukewarm

75 g (2½ oz) unsalted butter, melted
40 g (1½ oz/scant 3 tablespoons) lager beer
3 egg whites
icing (powdered) sugar, for dusting
Chantilly Cream or Hot Chocolate Sauce (*see pages 59 and 60*), to serve (*optional*)

CHEF'S TOUCHES

Of course, you can make the perfect-shaped rectangular waffle, *but it's quite fun and it looks great to have the odd quirky shape — or try pouring a nice round shape in the middle of the iron, making it look a bit more dramatic when served on a plate with sauces and garnishes.*

Because we love them really! Served with icing sugar on top, plenty of berries or some warm chocolate sauce, they are always a success story.

METHOD

MAKING THE WAFFLES

1. In a medium bowl, sift together the flour, salt and baking powder. In another bowl, whisk together the egg yolks, half the sugar and the vanilla extract, followed by the lukewarm milk, melted butter and lager. Whisk this into the sifted flour mixture, ensuring a smooth texture with no lumps.

2. Cover the bowl with cling film (plastic wrap) and leave to rest on the side for 1–1½ hours.

3. When you're ready to cook, heat the waffle iron for 5 minutes on each side over a low heat.

4. Meanwhile, whip the egg whites to firm peaks, gradually adding the remaining caster sugar from medium peaks stage onwards. Using a rubber spatula, fold the egg whites into the batter.

5. Away from the heat, lightly spray or brush the inside of the waffle iron with a little bit of vegetable oil and place back on the hob. Pour a ladle of batter into one side, covering the grid all over (*see Chef's Touches*). Close the iron securely. Flip over the iron to allow the mixture to flow through and nicely fill up both sides. Cook for 2½ minutes in total, flipping the iron halfway to get an even colour. If using an electric iron, follow the manufacturer's instructions.

6. Using a small palette or small knife, carefully take the waffles out of the iron and transfer it to a cooling rack. Keep warm while you make the rest, or eat them straight away, dusted generously with icing sugar.

TO SERVE

7. If you've managed to resist eating the waffles straight out of the iron, you can flash-heat your waffles in a hot iron for a few seconds to crisp them back up and give everyone the chance to eat them together. I usually eat them covered with icing sugar, but they also work a treat with hot chocolate sauce or Chantilly cream, or even with some fresh strawberries marinated in sugar with a dash of lemon juice.

le riz au lait

serves 6

PREPARATION TIME
5 minutes, plus 2 hours soaking

COOKING TIME
40–45 minutes

SPECIAL EQUIPMENT
Round shallow baking dish, about 16 cm (6¼ in) diameter,
4 cm (1½ in) deep

PLANNING AHEAD
Soak the rice in a large amount of cold water for about
2 hours prior to cooking. Pass the rice through a sieve and
rinse it well under a cold water tap for a couple of minutes,
removing as much starch as possible. Leave on the side
to drain.

INGREDIENTS

1.125 kg (2 lb 8 oz/4½ cups)
  organic whole milk
80 g (2¾ oz) caster
  (superfine) sugar
1 vanilla pod (bean), halved
  and scraped
70 g (2½ oz) pudding rice,
  soaked

fresh berries or a good
  homemade garden
  rhubarb compote,
  to serve (*optional*)

Technically not a bake, but I love making this
simple recipe for my friends. It is inspired by
both my mum and Raymond Blanc's mum
(Maman Blanc), as this dessert clearly holds a
special place in our hearts. It's my mum's
go-to dessert, which she is famous for in our
family. She caramelises the pudding with
caster sugar and a heated-up iron stick over
the open fire.

METHOD

1. In a medium thick-bottomed saucepan, combine the
   milk and sugar. Add the vanilla seeds and the split pod
   to the milk. Bring the milk to the boil over a medium
   heat, then add the drained pudding rice. Bring it back
   to the boil, stirring continuously with a large wooden
   spoon. When it's close to boiling over, reduce the heat
   to a gentle simmer and cook for 40–45 minutes,
   stirring every 3–4 minutes for the first 15–20 minutes.
2. When the consistency starts to thicken, stir every
   2 minutes to prevent the rice from sticking to the
   bottom of the saucepan. When the mixture is
   reaching a loose texture but the rice grains are fully
   cooked, pour it into the baking dish and leave to cool
   completely and set for a couple of hours. Serve with
   fresh berries or a good homemade garden rhubarb
   compôte, if you like.

CHEF'S TOUCHES

If you want to caramelise the top like my mum does, *when it's cool, sprinkle the top with caster sugar and caramelise it with a blowtorch.*
It's best to do this before the meal so the caramel has time to melt.

chocolate fondant

makes 6

This dessert has different names depending on where you come from. You may know it as molten or lava chocolate cake; I used to call it a chocolate fondant. It was one of the most popular restaurant desserts in the 80s and 90s, and I have been making and evolving it throughout my career. I like to serve it like we did back in the day at Le Manoir, with amaretto and pistachio ice cream!

PREPARATION TIME
15 minutes

COOKING TIME
12 minutes, plus 2 minutes resting

SPECIAL EQUIPMENT
6 foil pudding tins (6 x 4.5 cm/2½ x 1¾ in), probe thermometer, hand whisk, rubber spatula, squeezy bottle

PLANNING AHEAD
The fondant will need to be refrigerated for at least 2 hours. Both the fondant and vanilla crème anglaise can be prepared a couple of days in advance and kept in the refrigerator, ready to be used.

INGREDIENTS

60 g (2 oz/¼ cup) caster (superfine) sugar
15 g (½ oz/1 tablespoon) cocoa powder
50 g (1¾ oz) unsalted butter, softened
icing (powdered) sugar, for dusting
pistachio ice cream, to serve

For the fondant
35 g (1¼ oz/¼ cup) plain (all-purpose) flour
3 g (½ teaspoon) baking powder
130 g (4½ oz) 70% good-quality dark chocolate
60 g (2 oz) unsalted butter
3 small eggs (about 140 g/ 5 oz)
90 g (3¼ oz/¾ cup) icing (powdered) sugar
60 g (2 oz/¼ cup) double (heavy) cream

For the amaretto and chocolate cream
50 g (1¾ oz/scant ¼ cup) whipping cream
150 g (5½ oz/scant ⅔ cup) double (heavy) cream
25 ml (scant 2 tablespoons) amaretto or Disaronno
12 g (¼ oz) grated dark chocolate

For the pistachio sauce
200 g (7 oz) Vanilla Crème Anglaise (*see page 57*)
30 g (1 oz) Pistachio Paste (*see page 60*)

For the nuts
25 g (1 oz/¼ cup) flaked (slivered) almonds
25 g (1 oz/scant ¼ cup) shelled pistachios
dash of kirsch eau de vie
10 g (½ oz/2 teaspoons) icing (powdered) sugar

METHOD

LINING THE TINS
1. Whisk together the sugar and the cocoa powder. Brush a thin coating of softened butter all over the insides of the tins, then spoon the sugar and cocoa mixture all over the buttered insides. Leave to set in the refrigerator until needed.

MAKING THE FONDANT
2. Sift together the flour and the baking powder.
3. In a hot bain-marie, melt the chocolate with the butter until it reaches around 45°C (113°F).
4. In a separate bowl, whisk together the eggs, icing sugar and double cream. Whisk the melted butter and chocolate into the egg mixture, then gradually add the sifted flour mixture. Divide equally between the 6 pudding tins, ensuring the mixture only comes halfway up the sides (or put around 80 g/2¾ oz in each tin). Place in the refrigerator for at least 2 hours.

FOR THE AMARETTO & CHOCOLATE CREAM
5. In a medium bowl, combine all the ingredients, whisking for a couple of minutes to thicken slightly. Reserve in a small container in the refrigerator.

FOR THE PISTACHIO SAUCE
6. Whisk together the vanilla crème anglaise with the pistachio paste until smooth and set aside in the refrigerator, in a squeezy bottle if you have one or a small container.

TOASTING THE NUTS
7. Preheat the oven to 160°C fan (320°F).
8. In a medium bowl, combine both the almonds and pistachios with the kirsch eau de vie to dampen. Add the icing sugar and stir to coat the nuts.
9. Transfer the nuts onto a baking tray lined with baking parchment and toast in the oven for about 8 minutes. Set aside to cool.

BAKING & FINISHING

10. Increase the oven temperature to 170°C fan (340°F).
11. Arrange the completely cold fondant tins on a baking tray and bake for 12 minutes. Remove from the oven and leave to rest for 2 minutes before de-moulding.

12. Meanwhile, with a spoon, drizzle the amaretto cream in a zigzag across each serving plate. Pipe or spoon the pistachio paste into the gaps, and sprinkle the toasted nuts over the sauce on one side of the plate. De-mould the fondants on top of the sauce, opposite the nuts, and dust gently with icing sugar. Serve with pistachio ice cream.

hazelnut
paris—brest

serves 6

This dessert was created by a baker who wanted to celebrate the cycling race between Paris and Brest in Brittany. The circular shape of the dessert was supposed to represent the wheel of a bicycle. With this recipe adaptation, the shape of the choux pastry would give the rider a little bit of a bumpy ride, but is delicious nevertheless!

PREPARATION TIME
45 minutes

COOKING TIME
40 minutes

SPECIAL EQUIPMENT
Piping bag with 1 cm (½ in) plain nozzles and 12–15 cm (½–⅓ in) nozzles, food processor, mixer with whisk attachment

PLANNING AHEAD
You can make the pastry cream in advance and use the remainder for another recipe. The praline paste can also be made in advance and kept in an airtight container in the refrigerator. The craquelin discs can be made ahead too and stored in the refrigerator or the freezer.

INGREDIENTS

For the base
200 g (7 oz) Choux Pastry (*see page 34*)
icing (powdered) sugar, for dusting
8–9 x 3 cm (1¼ in) discs of Vanilla Craquelin (*see page 34*)

For the hazelnut praline paste
175 g (6 oz/1¼ cups) hazelnuts
175 g (6 oz/¾ cup) caster (superfine) sugar

2 small pinches of salt
8 g (¼ oz/1½ teaspoons) hazelnut oil

For the cream filling
180 g (6¼ oz) Pastry Cream (*see page 54*)
170 g (6 oz) hazelnut praline paste
15 ml (1 tablespoon) kirsch eau de vie
170 g (6 oz) unsalted butter, softened

CHEF'S TOUCHES

Secure the baking parchment in place *by adding weights in the corners so it doesn't fly over the pastry in the oven.*

You may want to add *shavings untoasted of hazelnuts, chocolate sauce, or the remaining crushed caramelised nuts.*

METHOD

MAKING THE CHOUX NECKLACE

1. Preheat the oven to 170°C fan (340°F) and fill a piping bag fitted with the 1 cm (½ in) plain nozzle with the choux.

2. On a flat tray lined with silicone baking parchment (*see Chef's Touches*) or a baking mat, place a 14 cm (5½ in) diameter ring. Sprinkle a little icing sugar over the top to lay a circular mark on the mat.

3. Using this mark as a guide, pipe 8 or 9 regular 3 cm (1¼ in) diameter domes to form a necklace of choux pastry, spacing the domes 5 mm (¼ in) apart from each other. This will leave space for the choux to expand, and the buns will stick to each other as they bake.

4. Place a 3 cm (1¼ in) disc of craquelin on each dome of choux pastry. Bake for 35–40 minutes. Set aside to cool.

FOR THE HAZELNUT PRALINE PASTE

5. Preheat the oven to 150°C fan (300°F) and line a baking tray with baking parchment. Scatter over the hazelnuts and roast for about 8 minutes. Set aside to cool.

6. Meanwhile, preheat a medium pan over a medium heat. When hot, gradually add the sugar and heat until it forms a light brown caramel. Pour this caramel over the hazelnuts and leave to cool and set. When cool, break up the nuts and caramel up and keep about 70 g (2½ oz) to use later. Using a food processor or good jug blender, blend the rest into a paste with the hazelnut oil and the salt. Set aside.

FOR THE CREAM FILLING

7. In the mixer, with the whisk attachment whisk the cold pastry cream until smooth. Add the cooled praline paste and kirsch and combine. Then whisk in the butter for a couple of minutes until smooth and aerated with a pipeable texture.

8. Transfer the praline cream into a piping bag fitted with a large (12–15 mm/½–⅝ in) plain nozzle.

FINISHING

9. Two-thirds of the way up, slice horizontally through the baked choux pastry necklace and place the top part carefully on the side. Pipe the praline paste onto the base of each choux bun. Pipe a generous dome of cream filling on top. Sprinkle over some of the reserved caramelised hazelnuts and place the top of the choux necklace back on. Place it in the refrigerator to set.

10. Just before serving, dust with icing sugar.

See step-by-step images overleaf

blackcurrant charlotte

A beautiful summery dish that can be made in advance. If you have enough equipment, you can double up the recipe and keep one in the freezer for next time.

serves 6

PREPARATION TIME
1 hour (including making the sponge)

COOKING TIME
8–10 minutes for the sponge

SPECIAL EQUIPMENT
Food processor or blender, 16 cm (6¼ in) cake ring, 4.5 cm (1¾ in) deep, piping bag and 1 cm (½ in) plain nozzle

PLANNING AHEAD
Make the sponge batter before you start.

For the Charlotte sponge
½ recipe of Biscuit Cuillère sponge batter (*see page 44*)
20–40 g (¾ –1½ oz/ 1½ tablespoons–⅓ cup) icing (powdered) sugar, for dusting

For the fruit purée and soaking syrup
70 g (2½ oz/⅓ cup) caster (superfine) sugar
50 g (1¾ oz/ 3½ tablespoons) water
350 g (12 oz) fresh or frozen blackcurrants, plus extra (*optional*) to decorate

For the mousse
150 g (5½ oz) fruit purée (*see left*)
1½ gelatine leaves, soaked in cold water for 10 minutes and drained
180 g (6 oz/¾ cup) whipping cream
30 g (1 oz/¼ cup) icing (powdered) sugar

For the glaze
80 g (2¾ oz) blackcurrant purée (*see left*)
1 gelatine leaf, soaked in cold water and drained

PREPARING THE FRUIT PURÉE & SOAKING SYRUP

1. In a medium saucepan, bring the sugar, water and blackcurrants to a simmer for 2–3 minutes. Reserve about 50 g (1¾ oz/3½ tablespoons) of the cooking syrup on the side for soaking the sponge later on. Blitz the remaining contents of the pan into a purée and pass through a sieve, then set aside.

MAKING THE BISCUIT CUILLÈRE SPONGE

2. Preheat the oven to 190°C fan (375°F).
3. Line a flat 40 cm x 25 cm (16 x 10 in) tray with baking parchment and draw two stencils on the back of the paper: a rectangle measuring 25 x 11 cm (10 x 4¼ in) and a disc 14 cm (5½ in) in diameter. Flip the paper over and you should be able to see the marks through it. Place it on the tray.
4. Using a piping bag with an 1 cm (½ in) plain nozzle, follow the stencil marks to pipe a spiral to form a 14 cm (5½ in) disc for the base of the Charlotte. Then, using the rectangle as a guide, pipe continuously, moving from side to side in a zigzag until you have filled the stencil (*see images on page 47*).
5. Dust the rectangle of sponge with the icing sugar and leave for 5 minutes, then dust again and bake both sponges for 8–10 minutes until light blonde with a spongy texture. Once cooked, leave to rest for 15 minutes, then peel away the baking parchment.

LINING THE CHARLOTTE

6. Place the cake ring on a flat tray lined with baking parchment.
7. Using a serrated knife, divide the rectangle of sponge lengthways and put both halves inside the cake ring, with the cut sides at the bottom and the icing sugar side facing out. Join them together, pushing them together tightly and trim the end with a pair of scissors if necessary to get a flush seal.

Method continued overleaf

8. Place the disc of sponge in the base of the ring and brush generously with the reserved syrup to thoroughly soak it. Set aside.

FOR THE MOUSSE

9. In a small saucepan or in a microwave, warm up 50 g (1¾ oz) of the fruit purée. Add the softened gelatine leaves and stir to dissolve. Transfer to a medium bowl and combine with the remaining 100 g (3½ oz) of cold fruit purée.

10. Whip the cream with the icing sugar until medium peaks form, then whisk in the purée until smooth. Using a rubber spatula, transfer the mousse into the Charlotte and level. Place the Charlotte in the refrigerator to set for at least 2–3 hours, or reserve in the freezer until needed (*see Chef's Touches*).

FINISHING & GLAZING

11. In a small saucepan, bring the 80 g (2¾ oz) fruit purée to a simmer, then add the softened and drained gelatine leaf. Allow to cool a little, then spoon the glaze over the top of the Charlotte. You can add a few whole blackcurrants on top for presentation if you like.

CHEF'S TOUCHES

If you use the entire biscuit cuillère sponge recipe, *it will be enough for two Charlottes, so you can freeze one for another time.*

If you want to freeze your dessert for another time, *follow the recipe up to and including step 10, then transfer to the freezer. Take the ring off after it has been frozen for a few hours and wrap tightly in cling film (plastic wrap). This is to prevent it from capturing any strong flavours from other food in your freezer.*

Allow the dessert to defrost overnight in the refrigerator before eating. *You can keep the glaze in the freezer separately in a small bag and finish the dessert on the day of serving.*

coffee & cardamom tiramisu

serves 8

PREPARATION TIME
20 minutes

SPECIAL EQUIPMENT
Mixer with whisk attachment, 18 cm (7 in) cake ring, 6 cm (2½ in) deep, pastry brush, piping bag with 8 mm (⅜ in) plain nozzle, blowtorch, disposable piping bag (optional, for a nice finish)

PLANNING AHEAD
Prepare two 17 cm (6½ in) discs of biscuit cuillère sponge and two thin 16 cm (6¼ in) chocolate discs in advance. The dessert itself can be made the day before serving, and it tastes even better the following day! Make the coffee infusion before starting.

INGREDIENTS

For the mascarpone mousse
3 egg yolks
30 g (1 oz/2 tablespoons) water
70 g (2½ oz/⅓ cup) caster (superfine) sugar
200 g (7 oz/scant 1 cup) whipping cream, plus 20 g (¾ oz/1½ tablespoons) for the gelatine
1 gelatine leaf, soaked in cold water and drained
10 g (½ oz/2 teaspoons) amaretto
200 g (7 oz) mascarpone

For soaking the sponge
220 ml (7½ fl oz/scant 1 cup) espresso coffee
5–6 cardamom pods, depending how much you like the flavour, crushed

For building and finishing the tiramisu
2 x 17 cm discs of Biscuit Cuillère Sponge (see page 44)
2 x thin 16 cm (6¼ in) dark chocolate discs (see page 64)
50 g (1¾ oz) mascarpone (optional)
20 g (¾ oz) cocoa powder, for dusting

I used to make a recipe similar to this when working at The Ritz in Paris. This might not be the classic tiramisu recipe, but it holds together nicely and tastes delicious with the addition of cardamom in the coffee.

METHOD

MAKING THE MASCARPONE MOUSSE

1. In the mixer, start whisking the egg yolks on a medium speed. Meanwhile, in a small saucepan over a medium heat, combine the water and sugar and bring to a rolling boil for 1 minute. Turn off the mixer then quickly pour the cooked syrup over the egg yolks and start whisking on high speed straight away, lifting the bowl of the mixer slightly to make sure the whisk is catching all the syrup. Continue whisking until this mixture (called a sabayon) thickens and becomes pale in colour.

2. Meanwhile, warm the 20 g (¾ oz) of whipping cream gently in the microwave or in a small pan over a low heat. Add the softened and drained gelatine leaf and let it dissolve. Set aside.

3. Whip the 200 g (7 oz) of whipping cream to medium to firm peaks, then reserve in the refrigerator.

4. Combine the gelatine cream with the amaretto, then whisk this into the cooled egg yolk sabayon. Whisk in the mascarpone, then fold in the whipped cream.

BUILDING THE TIRAMISU

5. Line a flat tray with baking parchment and place the 18 cm (7 in) cake ring on top. Set aside.

6. Warm up the espresso with the cardamom pods and leave to infuse for 2–3 minutes (see *Chef's Touches*). Pass through a sieve and keep the coffee on the side for soaking.

7. Place a sponge disc at the base of the cake ring, and brush generously with the coffee infusion (see *Chef's Touches*). Pour one-third of the mascarpone sabayon inside the ring, making sure it fills up any gaps around the soaked sponge and against the cake ring. Place the second disc of sponge on top, brush generously with the cardamom coffee and top with another third of the mascarpone mousse.

Method continued overleaf

8. Place a thin dark chocolate disc in the centre, then cover it with about 100 g (3½ oz) of the remaining mascarpone mousse. Place the second chocolate disc on top, then transfer to the refrigerator or freezer to set for about 30 minutes.

9. For the finishing touches, whisk together the remaining mascarpone mousse with the 50 g (1¾ oz) of mascarpone and keep in the refrigerator.

10. Meanwhile, prepare a disposable piping bag, cutting the tip diagonally to create a 1 cm (½ in) opening (*see Chef's Touches*). Take the remaining mascarpone mousse out of the refrigerator and whisk it until it becomes a pipeable texture, while remaining creamy. Fill up the piping bag and pipe irregular snaking shapes to cover the entire tiramisu top. Place back in the refrigerator to set completely. It will need a good couple of hours but ideally overnight.

FINISHING

11. Carefully transfer the tiramisu with the ring onto a serving dish, lifting the tiramisu with a large palette knife. Using a blowtorch, gently warm up the side of the ring to loosen and release it from the tiramisu. Using a small sieve, generously dust the cocoa powder all over the tiramisu.

CHEF'S TOUCHES

The longer you leave *the cardamom to infuse the coffee, the stronger it will get, so the timing is really up to you.*

The idea is to soak each sponge *with as much coffee as it can carry and soak the sponge all the way through.*

You can also do *something similar using a 6 mm/¼ in) round plain nozzle or by fairly lightly pushing on the tiramisu with a rubber spatula.*

chocolate & vanilla profiteroles

I have seen profiteroles filled with Chantilly cream and topped with a sweet, stodgy glaze too many times. Where I come from (and this is my preference), we serve them filled with ice cream and topped with a lot of warm chocolate sauce.

serves 6

PREPARATION TIME
20–25 minutes

COOKING TIME
30–32 minutes

SPECIAL EQUIPMENT
2–3 piping bags, large and medium fluted nozzle, 1 cm (½ in) plain nozzle, small ice-cream scoop, small serving jug, sauce boat for serving

PLANNING AHEAD
Find the best vanilla ice cream you can buy. Prepare the choux pastry and have a sheet of craquelin ready in sthe freezer.

INGREDIENTS

250 g (9 oz) Choux Pastry with ½ sheet of craquelin (*see page 34*)
300 g (10½ oz) good-quality vanilla ice cream (*optional*)
200 g (7 oz) Chantilly Cream (*see page 59* – optional)

To serve
300 g (10½ oz) Hot Chocolate Sauce (*see page 60*)
20 g (¾ oz/scant ¼ cup) flaked (slivered) almonds, toasted

METHOD

MAKING THE CHOUX BUNS

1. Preheat the oven to 170°C fan (340°F).
2. Fill a piping bag fitted with a 1 cm (½ in) plain nozzle with the choux pastry, then pipe 24 x 2 cm (¾ in) wide choux buns (about 6–8 g/¼ oz) each onto a non-stick baking tray, evenly spaced out from one another. Cut out 24 x 3 cm (1¼ in) discs of frozen craquelin and place on top of each choux bun. Bake for 30–32 minutes. Remove from the oven and set aside to cool.

FINISHING THE PROFITEROLES

3. There are two ways to fill your choux buns: the English way with Chantilly cream, or the French way with vanilla ice cream. Using a serrated knife, horizontally slice every bun two-thirds of the way up, creating a nice little round lid to sit on top of each roll. Place all your choux bun bases on a small flat tray that can fit in your refrigerator or freezer (depending on what you choose to use).
4. If using Chantilly cream, whip the Chantilly cream to firm peaks and, using a piping bag with a medium fluted nozzle, pipe a generous swirl of cream in each choux bun base. Cover with the choux pastry lids and transfer to the refrigerator until needed.
5. If using the ice cream, place the bun bases on the tray in the freezer to cool, then pipe your ice cream into them using the same method as for the Chantilly cream. If you have a small ice-cream scoop, you can simply place a small scoop of ice cream into each choux bun base instead. Do not top them with the lids yet; just place the ice-cream buns back in the freezer until needed. Reserve the lids on the side.

CHEF'S TOUCHES

You can build up a large sharing profiterole platter *instead of serving individually to create more of a centrepiece.*

SERVING THE PROFITEROLES

6. It's always nice to have some Chantilly cream available to serve with your profiteroles, even if you have filled them with ice cream.

7. Using a large fluted nozzle, pipe a dollop of Chantilly cream into the centre of each plate, then place three profiteroles around it, with a fourth one on top

(*see Chef's Touches*). You can pipe a bit more Chantilly in between the gaps or serve it on the side in a sauce boat. Drizzle some warm chocolate sauce over the top add a few toasted flaked almonds. Place a jug of hot chocolate sauce on the table so your guests can add more, and to bring a little theatre to proceedings!

strawberry financier

with lime, tonka bean & mascarpone cream

serves 6—8

PREPARATION TIME
30 minutes

COOKING TIME
16–18 minutes, plus 20 minutes cooling

SPECIAL EQUIPMENT
20 cm (8 in) tart ring, piping bag with plain 1 cm (1½ in) nozzle, hand whisk

PLANNING AHEAD
Before measuring the ingredients for the financier base, place a medium baking tray or similar, about 20 cm (8 in) square, in the freezer to stop the cooking of the butter when it's ready. You can also prepare the mascarpone cream and the fruit compote the day before to speed things up.

A lovely summer dessert to share with your friends ... and not that complicated, really.

INGREDIENTS

For lining the tart ring
20 g (¾ oz) unsalted butter, softened
20 g (¾ oz/1½ tablespoons) demerara sugar

For the financier base
90 g (3¼ oz) unsalted butter
65 g (2¼ oz/⅔ cup) round almonds
35 g (1¼ oz/2½ tablespoons) caster (superfine) sugar
105 g (3½ oz/generous ¾ cup) icing (powdered) sugar, sifted
45 g (1½ oz/⅓ cup) plain (all-purpose) flour
115 g (4 oz) egg whites
pinch of salt
½ teaspoon vanilla extract
dash of dark rum
5 large strawberries, thickly sliced

For the fruit compote
200 g (7 oz) fresh strawberries, blitzed into a purée

100 g (3½ oz) fresh raspberries
25 g (1 oz/scant 2 tablespoons) caster (superfine) sugar
15 g (½ oz/1 tablespoon) cornflour (cornstarch)
15 g (½ oz/1 tablespoon) lemon juice

For the lime and tonka mascarpone cream
250 g (9 oz/generous 1 cup) UHT whipping cream
½ vanilla pod (bean), split in half and the seeds scraped out
1 tonka bean
zest of ½ lime
25 g (1 oz/scant 2 tablespoons) icing (powdered) sugar
150 g (5½ oz) mascarpone

To decorate
250 g (9 oz) fresh strawberries, washed and quartered
a few lemon balm leaves (optional)

See method overleaf

MAKING THE FINANCIER BASE

1. Preheat the oven to 170°C fan (340°F). Place a 20 cm (8 in) square baking tray into the freezer.

2. In a small saucepan, cook the butter over a medium heat until it starts foaming and the foam becomes light brown in colour *(see Chef's Touches)*. Transfer it immediately into the frozen tray to stop the butter from cooking further and cool it down. Reserve on the side.

3. In a medium bowl, whisk together the ground almonds, caster sugar, icing sugar and flour, then set aside. In another medium bowl, whisk the egg whites by hand with a pinch of salt until soft peaks form. Add the flour, ground almond and sugar mixture, and fold in with the whisk. Whisk in the cooled butter and add the vanilla extract and rum. Place in the refrigerator to set slightly.

4. With your finger or a small brush, rub the inside of the tart ring with the softened butter and then dust with demerara sugar. On a flat baking tray, place the sugared tart ring on a slightly bigger square of baking parchment, which is on top of slightly larger square of foil. Roll the foil and paper in towards the ring to create a tight seal and prevent the mixture running away when baking later.

5. Pour the batter into the tart ring and arrange the thickly sliced strawberries all over the top. Bake for 18–20 minutes, or until the financier sponge is a nice golden colour. Remove from the oven, carefully peel off the foil and parchment, and remove the ring straight away before it starts sticking on the ring too much. Leave the financier to cool completely.

FOR THE FRUIT COMPÔTE

6. In a medium saucepan, bring the puréed strawberries, raspberries and sugar to the boil. Meanwhile, combine the cornflour and lemon juice in a small cup and pour this mixture into the pan. Quickly whisk together, then bring back to the boil and thicken for 1 minute, whisking continuously. Transfer the compôte into a bowl and let it cool completely to set. Reserve in the refrigerator until needed.

FOR THE LIME & TONKA MASCARPONE CREAM

7. In a medium saucepan, warm 100 g (3½ oz) of the whipping cream with the split and scraped vanilla pod. Remove from the heat and, using a thin grater, grate in the tonka bean and lime zest, then stir to combine and leave to infuse and cool on the side for 10–15 minutes *(see Chef's Touches)*.

8. In a medium bowl, combine the icing sugar, mascarpone cheese and remaining whipping cream. Set aside in the refrigerator. When the cream infusion has cooled, remove the vanilla pod and add the infusion to the mascarpone and sugar mixture. Combine briefly with a whisk and reserve in the refrigerator, covered, until needed.

FINISHING

9. Before the meal or 2 hours before serving, remove the cream from the refrigerator and whisk it until medium peaks just form. Transfer to a piping bag with a 1 cm (½ in) plain nozzle, then pipe a necklace of mascarpone cream, in round, pointy petals, around the top of the financier base. Spoon the cold and set fruit compôte into the centre and continue piping with more cream to cover it completely. Finish with the strawberry quarters, placing them elegantly all over the dessert, and a few lemon balm leaves if you have any.

This stage is called noisette or hazelnut butter *as it develops a nutty smell and taste and becomes a golden-brown colour. Cooking the butter further, or letting it become dark at the bottom of the pan, would create bitterness, and it would not smell and taste nutty as it should.*

If tonka is not your thing, *add sherry to the mascarpone instead and do not warm up the cream with the vanilla.*

hot soufflés

makes 4

PREPARATION TIME
15 minutes

COOKING TIME
8–10 minutes

SPECIAL EQUIPMENT
4–5 large (9 cm/3½ in diameter) tea cups, 6 cm (2½ in) deep, or similar size soufflé ramekins, soft brush, small sieve

PLANNING AHEAD
You can line and prepare your soufflés cups in advance and have them ready in the refrigerator. Prepare the pastry cream in advance. You can also prepare all your basic ingredients, except for the egg whites and sugar, so that you have them weighed and ready to go.

INGREDIENTS

For lining the soufflé cups
30 g (1 oz) unsalted butter, softened
100 g (3½ oz/scant ½ cup) caster (superfine) sugar

For raspberry soufflés
125 g (4½ oz) Pastry Cream (*see page 54*)
75 g (2½ oz) fresh raspberries
150 g (5½ oz) egg whites
75 g (2½ oz/⅓ cup) caster (superfine) sugar
icing (powdered) sugar, for dusting

For pistachio soufflés
125 g (4½ oz) Pastry Cream (*see page 54*)
75 g (2½ oz) Pistachio Paste (*see page 60*)
150 g (5½ oz) egg whites
75 g (2½ oz/⅓ cup) caster (superfine) sugar
icing (powdered) sugar, for dusting

For vanilla soufflés
185 g (6 oz) Pastry Cream (*see page 54*)
15 g (½ oz/1 tablespoon) vanilla extract
150 g (5½ oz) egg whites
75 g (2½ oz/⅓ cup) caster (superfine) sugar
icing (powdered) sugar, for dusting

For Grand Marnier soufflés
150 g (5½ oz) Pastry Cream (*see page 54*)
50 g (1¾ oz/3½ tablespoons) Grand Marnier
150 g (5½ oz) egg whites
75 g (2½ oz/⅓ cup) caster (superfine) sugar
icing (powdered) sugar, for dusting

ice cream or sorbet of your choice, to serve (optional)

This true showstopper dessert impresses every guest. For best results, I would recommend using only fresh egg whites. For this recipe, I've included four different flavours to try.

METHOD

LINING THE SOUFFLÉ CUPS
1. Brush the inside of each cup or mould with the softened butter, finishing by brushing the sides upwards to even out the butter. Pour the sugar into the first cup and rotate until completely coated, then tip the excess into the next one. Repeat for every cup and then place them in the refrigerator to set.

MAKING THE SOUFFLÉS
2. Preheat the oven to 170°C fan (340°F) with a flat baking tray inside.
3. In a large bowl, whisk the pastry cream until smooth. Add your chosen flavouring and whisk to combine (*see Chef's Touches*).
4. Whip the egg whites to medium to firm peaks, gradually adding the sugar from soft peaks stage onwards (*see Chef's Touches*). Using a hand whisk, add one-third of the egg white into the pastry cream mixture and whisk quickly to combine until smooth (*see Chef's Touches*).
5. Now, using a rubber spatula, carefully fold in the remaining whipped egg whites until fully combined. Divide the mixture between the cups, filling each one to the top. Using a palette knife, level and smooth the surface, then dust all over with a thin coating of icing sugar.
6. Holding the rim of the mould with your thumb and index finger, and without squeezing too hard, circle the cup, removing about 2–3 mm (1/16 in) of mixture from the edge to prevent the soufflé sticking to the side when rising in the oven (*see Chef's Touches*).

BAKING
7. Place each soufflé in the microwave for 5–10 seconds maximum, or until the top part of each soufflé is slightly domed. This will help them to rise nicely in the oven.
8. Space out the soufflés on the hot baking tray and bake for 10–12 minutes until nicely risen.
9. Serve with ice cream or sorbet if you like.

See step-by-step images overleaf

You can prepare this in advance *and keep in the refrigerator until needed.*

Whipping your egg whites *to the right consistency is important to get a beautiful lift and a creamy texture inside the*

soufflés. It should be firm but supple — when you lift out your whisk, the meringue should stay with it but the tip should still have some movement. This lightens the mixture and also eases the incorporation of the remaining egg white.

When you master your technique, *you can prepare your soufflés and have them ready to bake, keeping them in the freezer for up to 1 hour. You may need to give them an extra second in the microwave before baking them.*

petits
gateaux

CHAPTER 7

blueberry &
kirsch tartlets

serves 6

One of my favourite little desserts, bringing back memories of Auvergne in France, where the bakeries serve large slices of tart, covered with pastry cream and freshly picked blueberries. I personally prefer using wild blueberries, but with the season being very short, I've adapted this recipe to use regular blueberries.

PREPARATION TIME
20 minutes

COOKING TIME
20 minutes

SPECIAL EQUIPMENT
6 cm (2½ in) non-stick brioche moulds, or any tartlet/muffin moulds you may have, set of plain cutters, size depending on which moulds you use, piping bag and small plain nozzle, small pastry brush

PLANNING AHEAD
Prepare the sablé pastry to the point of rolling out. Prepare the almond cream and pastry cream.

INGREDIENTS

plain (all-purpose) flour, for dusting
200 g (7 oz) Sablé Pastry (see page 24)
unsalted butter, softened, for greasing
60 g (2 oz) Almond Cream (see page 56)
120 g (4¼ oz) small fresh blueberries, or wild blueberries, if you can find them
80 g (2¾ oz) Pastry Cream (see page 54)
5 g (¼ oz/1 teaspoon) kirsch eau de vie (to your taste)

icing (powdered) sugar, for dusting

For the blueberry glaze
100 g (3½ oz) best-quality blueberry jam you can find

Or, to make your own glaze
140 g (5 oz/scant ⅔ cup) blueberry juice
6 g (¼ oz) potato flour or cornflour (cornstarch)
½ gelatine leaf, soaked in cold water and drained

METHOD

PREPARING THE TARTLET CASES

1. On a well-floured table, roll out the sablé pastry to about 2.5 mm (⅙ in) thick and cut out six discs using a plain cutter big enough to line your moulds (see Chef's Touches). Lightly brush a bit of softened butter into tartlet moulds, then line them with the pastry discs, making sure no air pockets get trapped at the bottom. Use a small paring knife to cut away any excess pastry from around the edges of the mould.

2. Preheat the oven to 170°C fan (340°F).

3. Using a piping bag with a medium plain nozzle, pipe 8–10 g (¼–½ oz) almond cream into the centre of each tartlet case. Bake the tartlets on a baking tray for about 20 minutes, or until nicely golden brown in colour. Remove from the oven and cool for 5–10 minutes. Pop the tartlet cases out of the moulds before the fat sets and makes it tricky. If struggling, gently tap each mould on its side, as this helps to release the vacuum. Leave to cool completely.

MAKING THE GLAZE

4. If you haven't found a nice blueberry jam, then whisk together the blueberry juice and cornflour in a small saucepan. Bring to the boil to thicken for 30 seconds, whisking continuously, then add the drained, softened, gelatine leaf and transfer into a small bowl. Set aside to cool.

BUILDING THE TARTLETS

5. Wash the blueberries and drain over a clean, dry towel. In a medium bowl, whisk the pastry cream to soften and add the kirsch eau de vie. Transfer into a piping bag with a small plain nozzle.

CHEF'S TOUCHES

For 6 cm (2½ in) brioche moulds, an 8–9 cm (3¼–3½ in) cutter will be fine.

You can use a similar method with any fruit variation you want, such as strawberries or raspberries. You can

also pipe some of the lemon cream from the Lemon and Grapefruit Dacquoise (see page 234) on top of the tart.

6. Dab a small amount of blueberry juice or melted blueberry jam on top of the baked almond cream, ensuring it doesn't bleed onto the edges of the tartlets.

7. Pipe about 10 g (½ oz) of the kirsch pastry cream on top. In another medium bowl, warm the blueberry jam or the glaze in the microwave for a few seconds, then toss in the blueberries. With a fork or small spoon, arrange the blueberries on top of the cream so you have a nice dome of blueberries, as per the photo.

8. If you have some spare blueberries that have not been glazed, you can cut two or three in half and add them, sliced side facing upwards, to create a nice little contrast. To finish, using a small sieve, dust a little bit of icing sugar around the edge of each tartlet.

summer berry jésuites

serves 12

These are so called because they look a little bit like the triangular pointy hats worn by Jesuit priests. I made these as a baker's apprentice back in France, and still find them absolutely beautiful to eat. My favourite part is the very crispy baked icing top. For this recipe, I fill them with a kirsch diplomat cream and some fresh seasonal berries after baking.

PREPARATION TIME
25 minutes

COOKING TIME
25 minutes

SPECIAL EQUIPMENT
Mixer with whisk attachment

PLANNING AHEAD
Prepare the puff pastry in advance (laminated and rested) and make space in the refrigerator.

INGREDIENTS

For the pastry triangles
300 g (10½ oz) Quick
  Puff Pastry (*see page 30*)
30 g (1 oz/⅓ cup) flaked
  (slivered) almonds

For the icing
20 g (¾oz) egg whites
100 g (3½ oz/generous
  ¾ cup) icing (powdered)
  sugar, sifted
dash of lemon juice or white
  wine vinegar

For the diplomat cream filling
300 g (10½ oz) Pastry
  Cream (*see page 54*)
10 g (½ oz/2 teaspoons)
  kirsch eau de vie
50 g (1¾ oz) whipped cream

For filling and serving
100 g (3 ½ oz) strawberries
100 g (3 ½ oz) raspberries
50 g (1¾ oz) blueberries
50 g (1¾ oz) blackberries
icing (powdered) sugar, to
  decorate
mixed berry coulis, to serve

METHOD

1. Roll out the puff pastry into a rectangle about 25 x 23 cm (10 x 9 in), 4 mm (¼ in) thick. Transfer the dough onto a cold tray and rest flat in the refrigerator for 30 minutes.

ICING

2. Meanwhile, whisk together the egg whites, icing sugar and lemon juice until the mixture firms up and peaks a little to achieve a spreadable paste texture.

3. Remove the pastry from the refrigerator and, using a palette knife, quickly and evenly spread the icing all over the pastry. Dip a long kitchen knife in cold water to dampen and divide the very cold pastry lengthways to create two strips approx. 12 cm (4½ in) each . Use the same knife to trim the rough edge of each band.

4. Line a baking tray with baking parchment. Dampening the knife as above, cut each strip of puff pastry into 6 triangles, 7 cm (2¾ in) wide. Arrange the triangles on the prepared baking tray, leaving at least a 3–4 cm (1¼–1½ in) gap between them. Sprinkle the flaked almonds on top and leave the triangles to dry out in the refrigerator for 30 minutes.

5. Preheat the oven to 170°C fan (340°F).

6. Bake for about 10 minutes. You will need a raised cooling rack sitting about 4 cm (1½ in) high (*see Chef's Touches*). Place a sheet of silicone baking parchment on top to prevent the pastry triangles flipping over and to keep them level. Bake for a further 15 minutes until nice and golden.

7. Remove from the oven, remove the rack and parchment and leave to cool.

CHEF'S TOUCHES

To bake the Jésuites, *you'll need four 4 cm (1½ in) tall objects that you have and that are suitable to heat in the oven, placing one in* *each corner of the baking tray. Ideal objects are dariole moulds or coffee cups, or you can stack a couple of moulds together.*

MAKING THE DIPLOMAT CREAM & FINISHING

8. Soften the pastry cream with a whisk until smooth.
Add the kirsch eau de vie and fold in the whipped
cream. Carefully divide each cooled Jésuite in half
so you have a top and a bottom. Set aside the iced top
parts (they are very fragile). Hollow out the centre of
the base of each, cutting out a little of the soft pastry
in the middle to create a gap. Using a 1 cm (½ in) nozzle,
pipe the cream inside this gap and around the edge.

9. Quickly wash the berries in cold water and drain.
Remove the strawberry stems and halve some of the
raspberries and blackberries. The strawberries can
be quartered or sliced, it's up to you.

10. Top the Jésuites with the mixed berries, sprinkle over
a little icing sugar and place the iced lids back on.

11. Serve with a mixed berry coulis.

macarons

makes 30

A traditional Parisian macaron recipe which shows off the skills of any home baker.

PREPARATION TIME
30 minutes, plus 30 minutes cooling

COOKING TIME
12 minutes

SPECIAL EQUIPMENT
Mixer with whisk attachment, temperature probe, hand blender, piping bag with 1 cm (½ in) plain nozzle

PLANNING AHEAD
Before enjoying your macaron, it is good practice to leave them in the refrigerator overnight, covered in a box, to allow the centre with the filling to become tender while the shell remains crispy.

INGREDIENTS

For the macaron paste
185 g (6½ oz/1½ cups) icing (powdered) sugar
185 g (6½ oz/generous 1¾ cups) ground almonds
70 g (2½ oz) fresh egg whites

For the macarons
75 g (2½ oz) fresh egg whites (*see Chef's Touches*)
50 g (1¾ oz) water
185 g (6½ oz/generous ¾ cup) caster (superfine) sugar

For a liquorice ganache filling
100 g (3½ oz/scant ½ cup) whipping cream
20 g (¾ oz) good-quality soft and sweet liquorice, finely chopped (*see Chef's Touches*)
90 g (3¼ oz) white chocolate, roughly chopped

For a dark chocolate ganache filling
100 g (3½ oz/scant ½ cup) whipping cream
100 g (3½ oz) good-quality dark chocolate (70% cocoa)

METHOD

FOR THE PASTE
1. Sift the icing sugar into a large bowl, then whisk in the ground almonds to break down any lumps. Add the egg whites and stir to form a paste. (You can add some coffee extract or colouring at this stage if you need it – *see Chef's Touches*).

MAKING THE MACARONS
2. Preheat the oven to 150°C fan (300°F).
3. Place the egg whites in the mixer bowl ready with the whisk attachment. In a small saucepan, heat the water, and the sugar over a medium heat. When it reaches 108°C (226°F), start to whisk the egg whites at a fast speed. When the sugar syrup reaches 117°C (243°F), quickly turn off the mixer and pour in the sugar syrup. Start the mixer again on full power straight away, lifting the bowl slightly to catch the syrup at the bottom for a few seconds. Continue whisking for a couple of minutes until the meringue firms up.
4. Using a wooden spoon, break down the macaron paste, adding a quarter of the warm meringue, mixing briskly to loosen the paste. Now, using a rubber spatula, gently fold in the remaining meringue. Fill a piping bag fitted with a plain nozzle with the mixture. Line a flat baking tray with silicone baking mats and pipe 3 cm (1¼ in) discs, 3 cm (1¼ in) apart, to allow the macarons to expand when baking. Bake for 12–14 minutes. Leave to cool on the side.

MAKING THE GANACHE
5. In a small pan, bring the cream to the boil (cook it with the chopped liquorice or the instant coffee, if using). Place the roughly chopped chocolate into a small jug and pour over the hot cream. Blend together straight away using a hand blender, then leave to cool on the side.

FINISHING THE MACARONS
6. When cooled, carefully peel off the macaron shells from the baking mat and place them, flat sides up, in similar-sized pairs on a flat tray. Fill a piping bag fitted with a medium plain nozzle with the ganache filling and pipe a small dome on one shell of each pair. Flip the remaining empty shell on top of the chosen filling and press gently to sandwich together.

You can add 10 g (½ oz) coffee extract *to the macaron paste if you want to flavour it, or add a few drops of food colouring if you want to reflect the flavour of your fillings, such as yellow for lemon.*

If you do not like liquorice, *you can replace the liquorice with 1 teaspoon good-quality instant coffee.*

You can also use *lemon cream, buttercream flavoured with vanilla or Coffee Extract (see page 71), Pistachio Paste (see page 60), jams and other curds to fill your macarons.*

polonaise brioche

serves 8

PREPARATION TIME
20 minutes

COOKING TIME
12 minutes

SPECIAL EQUIPMENT
Pastry brush, piping bag with medium plain nozzle, mixer with whisk attachment, temperature probe

PLANNING AHEAD
Save some brioche rolls from your previous batch. Make the pastry cream.

This translates to Polish brioche, but I'm not sure why. When I was an apprentice, it featured every day alongside coffee éclairs and religieuse, and was amongst our most popular items. We used unsold brioche rolls (*see page 106*) from the day before to make them.

1. Combine the sugar syrup, water and alcohol and set aside. Slice each baked brioche rolls horizontally into three equal slices. Using a pastry brush, generously soak each slice with the syrup.
2. In a large bowl, whisk the pastry cream until smooth and creamy. Add the alcohol and fold in the candied fruits. Transfer to a piping bag with a medium plain nozzle and pipe about 15 g (½ oz) of the cream over the bottom two slices of each brioche, leaving the rounded tops without. Rebuild each brioche roll by stacking up the bottom two slices with the pastry cream first, and finishing with the rounded top. Press gently on each brioche and transfer to the freezer for at least 30 minutes to firm up and make them easier to dip in the meringue.

MAKING THE MERINGUE

3. Preheat the oven to 180°C fan (350°F) and line a flat baking tray with baking parchment.
4. Meanwhile, in the bowl of the mixer, whisk together by hand the egg whites and sugar. Place over a bain-marie and whisk by hand continuously until the mixture heats up to about 60°C (140°F) (*see Chef's Touches*). Return the bowl to the mixer with the whisk attachment and whisk for a couple of minutes on full speed, or until it forms firm but supple peaks.
5. Prepare a small bowl with the flaked almonds on the side and take the brioches out of the freezer. Remove the bowl from the mixer and place it next to your brioche. Dip each roll into the meringue so the top three-quarters are coated, rotating the rolls in the meringue to cover them nicely. Scatter over the flaked almonds and place each coated brioche, meringue facing up, on the prepared baking tray, nicely spread apart. Using a small sieve, lightly dust with icing sugar.
6. Place in the oven for 5 minutes, then turn the tray around and bake for a further 5 minutes. Then turn off the oven and leave for a further 2 minutes. The meringue needs to be nicely baked with a golden brown colour all over. Remove from the oven and leave to cool.

For the soaking syrup
130 g (4½ oz/generous ½ cup) Sugar Syrup (*see page 70*)
40 g (1½ oz/scant 3 tablespoons) water
15 g (½ oz/1 tablespoon) kirsch eau de vie or dark rum

15 ml (1 tablespoon) kirsch eau de vie or dark rum
50 g (1¾ oz) candied fruit cubes or candied peel

For the Swiss meringue
70 g (2½ oz) egg whites
120 g (4¼ oz/½ cup) caster (superfine) sugar

For building the brioche
8 x 30 g (1 oz) baked Little Brioche Rolls (*see page 106*)
220 g (8 oz) Pastry Cream (*see page 54*)

To decorate
20 g (¾ oz/scant ¼ cup) flaked (slivered) almonds
15 g (½ oz/1¾ tablespoons) icing (powdered) sugar

If you don't have a temperature probe, *you can judge this stage by when it starts to feel too hot to keep the tip of your finger in.*

coffee éclairs

makes 12–14

PREPARATION TIME
40 minutes, plus cooling

COOKING TIME
35 minutes

SPECIAL EQUIPMENT
2 piping bags, plain or fluted 12 mm (½ in) nozzle, 6–8 mm (¼–⅜ in) plain nozzle, pointy nozzle, non-stick baking tray or mat

PLANNING AHEAD
You can make the éclairs a few hours in advance and keep them in the refrigerator. Empty baked choux pastry éclairs can also be stored in an airtight container in the freezer.

INGREDIENTS

For the éclairs
250–300g (9–10½ oz) Choux Pastry (*see page 34*)
400–450g (14 oz–1 lb) Pastry Cream (*see page 54*)
15–20 g (½–¾ oz) good-quality coffee extract (*see page 71* or use store-bought – *see Chef's Touches*)

For the glaze
200 g (7 oz) white pastry fondant (*see Chef's Touches*)
8–10 g (¼–½ oz) water
6–10 g (¼–½ oz) good quality coffee extract (*see page 71* or use store-bought)

I really love this one. When I go to France, for lunch we typically buy a selection of petits gateaux, which usually includes a couple of coffee éclairs. And guess what? As beautiful as the other petit gateaux can be, who will eat the éclairs comes down to who gets the first draw!

METHOD

1. Preheat the oven to 170°C fan (40°F).
2. Make half a recipe of choux pastry without the vanilla craquelin. Fill a piping bag fitted with a 12 mm (½ in) nozzle pipe 12–14 éclairs about 11 cm (4½ in) long, spaced well apart, across a non-stick baking tray. Bake in the middle of the oven for 35 minutes, without opening the door (*see Chef's Touches*). Remove from the oven and leave the éclairs to cool on the side.
3. Meanwhile, soften the cold pastry cream with a hand whisk or in a mixer for a couple of minutes, just enough to break down any lumps and achieve a smooth and creamy texture. Whisk in the coffee extract and transfer the coffee cream into a piping bag fitted with a 6–8 mm (¼–⅜ in) plain nozzle. Set aside.
4. Using the pointy tip of a small nozzle, pierce the underside of each éclair in three places along its length. Gently fill each éclair with the coffee cream.

PREPARING THE GLAZE

5. Place a small saucepan that's wide enough to dip the éclairs in over a low heat and gently warm the fondant with the water. Stir with a small wooden spoon and melt together gradually until lukewarm or about 35°C (95°F) (*see Chef's Touches*). Add the coffee extract according to taste and the strength of the extract.
6. One at a time, dip the top of each éclair into the warm glaze, then wipe off any excess with your finger (*see Chef's Touches*). Place the glazed éclairs on a serving dish in the refrigerator for a minimum of 30 minutes before serving.

See images and Chef's Touches overleaf

Sourcing a good-quality coffee extract will make a big difference to the flavours of your éclairs. *Alternatively, there's a recipe to make one in this book — see page 71. You can also replace some of the milk with espresso coffee or add coffee granules to the milk when making the pastry cream.*

You can now buy white pastry fondant *in specialist cake decorating shops. It is a crystallised sugar syrup solution. If you cannot find any, you can make this recipe using white ready-to-roll fondant icing, which you can treat the same way, but you will need to use twice the amount of water and a bit more coffee extract to get the right glazing colour and consistency.*

Opening the door of the oven *without first securing a firm crust on the éclairs will make them collapse straight away, and you will not be able to get them to rise back up.*

When preparing the glaze, 35°C (95°F) is the perfect temperature to get a slightly loose yet paste-like texture, *making it easy to glaze the éclairs. If you warm up your fondant too much, it will liquify and decrystallise, and you will have to start again or add more fresh fondant.*

Alternatively, you can pipe the glaze on top of the éclairs, *using a piping bag fitted with a 15 mm (⅝ in) wide flat nozzle.*

If you've baked too many éclairs, *you can freeze the empty shells and use the following week, though the quality of the pastry will be a bit drier.*

You can change your éclairs to chocolate, *flavouring the pastry cream with good-quality cocoa powder and 20 g (¾ oz) melted bitter dark chocolate. The amount of cocoa powder will depend on how strong you want the flavour to be. Combine the melted chocolate with the pastry cream when it is still a bit warm.*

the opéra petit gâteau

serves 8

PREPARATION TIME
40–50 minutes, plus 2 hours setting

COOKING TIME
10 minutes

SPECIAL EQUIPMENT
Mixer with whisk attachment, jug blender, two 38 x 26 cm (15 x 10½ in) very flat and level baking trays, pastry brush, temperature probe, pipng bag and small nozzle or paper cornet

PLANNING AHEAD
Make the espresso coffee 1 hour before building the gâteau to allow it to cool, and prepare the buttercream.

INGREDIENTS

For the coffee and almond sponge
70 g (2½ oz) egg whites
25 g (1 oz/scant 2 tablespoons) caster (superfine) sugar
110 g (3¾ oz) eggs
60 g (2 oz/½ cup) icing (powdered) sugar
15 g (½ oz) soft unsalted butter
85 g (3 oz/¾ cup) ground almonds
25 g (1 oz/scant ¼ cup) plain (all-purpose) flour, sifted
6 g (¼ oz) instant coffee
100 ml (3½ fl oz/scant ½ cup) cold espresso coffee, for soaking

For the coffee buttercream
150 g (5½ oz) Buttercream (*see page 58*)
10 g (½ oz) Coffee Extract (*see page 71* or use store-bought)

For the chocolate ganache
90 g (3¼ oz/generous ⅓ cup) whipping cream
70 g (2½ oz) dark chocolate (ideally 70% cocoa), roughly chopped
5 g (¼ oz) unsalted butter

For the chocolate glaze
150 g (5½ oz) good-quality dark chocolate (60% cocoa or more)
20 g (¾ oz/1½ tablespoons) sunflower oil or similar

If, like me, you love the flavour combination of coffee and chocolate, an opéra petit gâteau is the *nec plus ultra* dessert. Named after the Opéra Garnier in Paris and created at a time when refrigeration was not yet commonly used to make desserts or pastries, it is made with rich almond sponge, coffee buttercream and chocolate ganache. When made correctly, what should be a very heavy and rich cake to eat magically disappears in your mouth like the sweetest of treats, with a taste to come back to. I love it!

METHOD

MAKING THE SPONGE

1. Preheat the oven to 200°C fan (400°F).
2. Add the egg whites to the bowl of a mixer with a whisk attachment and keep the caster sugar on the side. Separately, in a jug blender, blitz together all the remaining sponge ingredients except the espresso on full blast for 8–10 minutes. Transfer to a medium bowl. Now, whisk the egg whites to soft peaks and gradually add the caster sugar. Continue whisking until firm peaks form.
3. Whisk a quarter of the whipped egg whites into the almond mixture and knock it down vigorously to loosen. Using a rubber spatula, gently fold this back into the mixer bowl with the remaining whipped egg whites until fully combined (*see Chef's Touches*).
4. Line one of the flat trays with baking parchment. Pour over the sponge mixture and spread evenly with a palette knife. Bake for about 10 minutes (*see Chef's Touches*). When baked, slide the sponge with the baking parchment onto a cooling rack to cool.

MAKING THE COFFEE BUTTERCREAM

5. In a medium bowl, whisk together the soft buttercream and the coffee extract and set aside.

FOR THE DARK CHOCOLATE GANACHE

6. In a small pan over a medium heat, bring the cream to a quick boil and pour it over straight over the chopped dark chocolate in a heatproof bowl. Whisk together until fully combined. Allow to cool for 5–10 minutes, then stir in the butter. Set aside.

BUILDING THE OPÉRA

7. Cut the sponge sheet into three equal strips, each measuring 22 x 11 cm (8½ x 4¼ in).

8. Line a very flat tray with baking parchment or a plastic sheet. Add 80 g (2¾ oz) of the coffee buttercream and level with a palette knife so it's just slightly bigger than one of the sponge strips. Place one sponge strip on top, upside down, and gently press the spare flat baking tray on top to level. Remove the spare tray and, using a pastry brush, soak the top of the sponge with one-third of the cold espresso coffee.

9. Top with another 60 g (2 oz) coffee buttercream and spread this with the palette knife to the edges of the sponge. Place another strip of sponge on top and again gently press with the spare flat tray to level. Repeat the soaking with another third of the coffee. Now pour and evenly spread 60–80 g (2–2¾ oz) of the chocolate ganache on top and cover it with the last sponge strip. Gently press again with the flat tray and soak the sponge with the remaining coffee. Place the cake in the refrigerator for a couple of hours to set.

FINISHING & GLAZING THE OPÉRA

10. Take the cold cake out of the refrigerator and lay a sheet of baking parchment on top. Place the spare flat tray on top of the paper to sandwich the gâteau and flip over both trays. Lift off what used to be the base tray and peel off the baking parchment or plastic sheet, which should leave you with a level, flat coffee buttercream layer that is exposed and ready to be glazed.

11. Now prepare the glaze. Slowly melt the chocolate with the vegetable oil in the microwave until it reaches about 40°C (104°F). Transfer the glaze into a small jug and get a large palette knife ready. Quickly pour the glaze all over the gâteau and use the palette knife to spread it out to 1–2 mm (1/32–1/16 in) thick before it sets. Leave the glaze to completely set, then trim the edges neatly using a hot serrated knife heated up in a tall jug of hot water or warmed with a blowtorch.

12. At this stage, divide and mark the gateau into 5 cm (2 in) square portions with the hot knife. Now fully cut each slice, using the hot knife to get a clean cut (*see Chef's Touches*).

13. Using a small piping nozzle or a paper cornet, you can write the word, Opéra, on top of each petit gâteau, using any leftover chocolate ganache.

CHEF'S TOUCHES

Fold the mixture into the egg whites gently, *retaining as much volume as possible to create a light sponge.*

The sponge is ready *when it springs back when pushed gently with your finger.*

Wipe the blade with a damp clean kitchen cloth *after each cut to get a neat slice.*

The opéra is even better a day later *and can be kept in the refrigerator for a few days. Just cover it tightly with cling film* *(plastic wrap) to avoid it drying out and losing its flavour.*

showstoppers

CHAPTER 8

pavlova

serves 6–8

PREPARATION TIME
40 minutes

COOKING TIME
1¾–2 hours

SPECIAL EQUIPMENT
2 disposable piping bags, ideally fitted with a Saint Honoré nozzle, or a piping bag that can be cut to imitate the famous quenelle shape, mixer with whisk attachment, flat baking tray

PLANNING AHEAD
You can prepare the coconut cream infusion a couple of hours in advance. You can also bake the pavlova base the day before serving, and keep it in a dry place.

INGREDIENTS

For the coconut cream
100 g (3½ oz/1 cup)
    desiccated (dried
    shredded) coconut
560 g (1 lb 4 oz/2½ cups)
    whipping cream
15 g (½ oz/1 tablespoon)
    caster (superfine) sugar
1 vanilla pod

For the pavlova meringue
100 g (3½ oz) egg whites
100 g (3½ oz/scant ½ cup)
    caster (superfine) sugar
100 g (3½ oz/generous
    ¾ cup) icing (powdered)
    sugar, sifted

For the garnish
2 kiwis
1 large ripe mango
1 passion fruit
20 g (¾ oz) apricot jam
2–3 sprigs of coriander
    (cilantro)

A few simple ingredients put together, and yet this dessert looks very impressive — and tastes delicious, of course. Feel free to use any fruit you like or that's in season.

METHOD

MAKING THE COCONUT CREAM

1. Place the desiccated coconut in a small non-stick frying pan (*see Chef's Touches*) over a low heat and cook for 2–3 minutes, stirring with a spoon every so often, until nicely toasted and golden brown in colour. Transfer it straight into a medium bowl and combine with the cold whipping cream. Leave to infuse for 30–40 minutes.

2. Pass through a sieve and discard the coconut. Combine the sugar with the cream. Split the vanilla pod lengthways and scrape the seeds only into the cream. Reserve in the refrigerator.

MAKING THE PAVLOVA MERINGUE

3. Preheat the oven to 90–100°C fan (200–210°F). Line a large flat baking tray with baking parchment. Prepare a piping bag with a Saint Honoré nozzle, or alternatively diagonally cut about 2 cm (¾ in) from the tip of a disposable piping bag with a pair of scissors, to create an angled piping shape.

4. In the mixer bowl, start whisking the egg whites, gradually adding the caster sugar from medium peak stage onwards. When firm peaks form, remove the bowl from the machine and gently fold in the icing sugar with a rubber spatula. Combine briefly until the icing sugar is incorporated (*see Chef's Touches*).

5. Fill the piping bag with the meringue and pipe a series of small petal-shaped quenelles of meringue, each about 3–4 cm (1¼–1½ in) long and 2 cm (¾ in) wide, in a straight line running the the length of the baking tray. The line should be about 35 cm (14 in) in length. Rotate the tray 180 degrees and pipe another line of quenelles, leaving a gap of 3–4 cm (1¼–1½ in) between the two lines. Now pipe 2–3 quenelles at each end to join the long lines together.

6. Bake the meringue in the oven for 1 hour 45 minutes to 2 hours, depending on how dry you want the meringue to be. Remove from the oven and leave on the side to cool completely, or in a dry place for the next day (*see Chef's Touches overleaf*).

Method continued overleaf

FINISHING THE PAVLOVA

7. Peel the kiwis, slice them into 1 cm (½ in) slices and cut each slice into quarters. Place in a bowl.

8. Peel the mango and cut half into 1–2 cm (½–¾ in) chunks. Add these to the bowl with the kiwis. Using a sharp knife, cut 8–10 nice wedges from the other mango half to decorate the dessert at the end. If you have any mango left, you can blitz the flesh into a nice coulis with any other leftover fruit to accompany the dessert later.

9. Cut the passion fruit in half, then remove the juice and seeds with a spoon and add the bowl of prepared fruit.

10. Melt the apricot jam in a microwave for few seconds and combine delicately with the fruits; without breaking them.

11. Finally, chop a small handful of coriander leaves and fold into the fruits, the quantity here is up to you.

ASSEMBLING THE DISH

12. Whisk the coconut cream to medium peaks and fill a piping bag. Pipe similar shape and size quenelles of cream in between the meringue ones, all around, and slightly offset, towards the centre. Cover any gaps in the centre of the meringue with 1 cm (½ in) of cream. Arrange the fruits harmoniously in the centre, finishing with the small wedges of mango and with a scattering of coriander.

CHEF'S TOUCHES

Ensure the pan is very clean *and free of any previous cooking scent, or this will be captured by the coconut and end up in your dessert.*

You're folding briefly here, *so stop as soon as the traces of icing sugar have disappeared. The more movement you add to the meringue, the shinier it will get, and the looser and softer the meringue will become, losing all structure and shape.*

This is the opposite of what we need on this occasion.

You can leave your meringue in the cold oven *if you want to finish it the next day, to keep it dry.*

chocolate crumble

lemon butterscotch & coffee chantilly cream

This crumble has been flipped on its head. You can make a simpler version by just making the chocolate crumble with the chocolate cream, and serving it with the lemon butterscotch sauce and the caramelised hazelnuts. It's still delicious, but less time-consuming.

serves 8

PREPARATION TIME
40 minutes, plus 3 hours setting time

COOKING TIME
12 minutes

SPECIAL EQUIPMENT
Mixer with a paddle attachment, 20 cm (8 in) tart ring, 18 cm (7 in) cake ring, blowtorch, piping bag and 1 cm (½ in) nozzle

PLANNING AHEAD
Prepare the lemon butterscotch sauce and chocolate pennies. The caramelised hazelnuts can also be made in advance and kept in an airtight container.

INGREDIENTS

For the cocoa crumble
35 g (1¼ oz/2½ tablespoons) demerara sugar
45 g (1½ oz/3 tablespoons) caster (superfine) sugar
pinch of salt
55 g (2 oz/½ cup) plain (all-purpose) flour
15 g (½ oz/1 tablespoon) cocoa powder
75 g (2½ oz) cold unsalted butter, cubed

For the chocolate cream
155 g (5½ oz) good-quality dark chocolate (70% cocoa), roughly chopped into small pieces
1 egg, beaten
165 ml (5½ fl oz/scant ¾ cup) whipping cream
70 ml (2½ fl oz/5 tablespoons) whole milk

For the coffee Chantilly cream
135 g (5 oz/generous ½cup) whipping cream
15 g (½ oz) coffee beans or ½ teaspoon good-quality instant coffee
⅓ gelatine leaf, soaked in cold water and drained
50 g (1¾ oz) milk chocolate

For the caramelised hazelnuts
20 g (¾ oz/1½ tablespoons) water
60 g (2 oz/generous ¼ cup) caster (superfine) sugar
100 g (3½ oz) peeled hazelnuts, crushed into chunks with a rolling pin
pinch of sea salt

To serve
100 g (3½ oz) Lemon Butterscotch Sauce (*see page 63*)
Chocolate Coins (*see page 64*)

See method overleaf

MAKING THE CRUMBLE

1. Preheat the oven to 170°C fan (340°F). In the mixer with the paddle attachment, mix together all the crumble ingredients, except the butter. Now add the cold butter cubes, and combine for a few minutes until you have a crumble texture (*see Chef's Touches*). Reserve the crumble in the fridge refrigerator or freezer for a minimum of 30 minutes before use using (*see Chef's Touches*).

2. Place the 20 cm (8 in) tart ring on a flat baking tray lined with baking parchment. Tip the crumble into the ring and spread it out evenly. Bake for 10-12 minutes (*see Chef's Touches*). Remove from the oven, carefully place the 18 cm (7 in) ring on top, press down slightly into the crumble without cutting through, and reserve on the side to cool.

MAKING THE CHOCOLATE CREAM

3. Place the chopped dark chocolate in a large bowl. In a separate, mediumbowl, beat the egg with a |whisk. In a small saucepan, bring the cream and milk to a quick boil, then whisk into the beaten egg. Pour this mixture onto the chopped chocolate and leave to melt for 1 minute, then whisk together until smooth. Pour this chocolate cream into the 18 cm (7 in) ring on top of the crumble and place the whole thing, including the tray, in the refrigerator to set for at least 2–3 hours.

MAKING THE COFFEE CHANTILLY CREAM

4. In a small saucepan, bring the cream to a quick boil and infuse the coffee beans for around about 15 minutes (*see Chef's Touches*). Reheat the cream and add the softened gelatine leaf to dissolve. Pass the infused cream through a sieve and weigh to ensure you have 135 g (5 oz).

5. In a small bowl, partially melt the milk chocolate in the microwave for 30 seconds or over a hot bain-marie. Gradually pour the hot coffee cream over the chocolate, whisking continuously until smooth. Cover and place in the refrigerator to cool and set for at least 2 hours.

MAKING THE CARAMELISED HAZELNUTS

6. In a medium saucepan, bring the water and sugar to the boil until it reaches about 115°C (239°F). Meanwhile, gently warm the cracked hazelnuts in the preheated oven for 2–3 minutes. Take the pan off the heat and, with a wooden spoon, quickly fold in the warm hazelnuts, along with the pinch of salt. The sugar will crystallise.

7. Return the pan to a medium heat and melt the sugar down gradually with the nuts so it turns into caramel. As soon as the hazelnuts are completely coated in the caramel, quickly tip them onto a non-stick baking tray lined with baking parchment and try to separate them with a spoon before they set. Allow to cool completely, then set aside in a small airtight container.

FINISHING THE CRUMBLE

8. Take the crumble out of the refrigerator and, using a large palette knife, carefully transfer it onto a flat serving dish. Now remove the rings. The outer ring should come off easily. If not, warm it up a little using a blowtorch. In the same way, warm up the middle ring just enough to slide it off the chocolate cream.

9. Briskly whisk the coffee Chantilly cream for 2–3 minutes to get a stable, pipeable texture. Fill a piping bag fitted with a 1 cm (½ in) nozzle with the cream. Pipe it randomly, in different-sized dots, all over the chocolate cream. Before serving the dessert, drizzle over some lemon butterscotch sauce, and place a few chocolate coins on the coffee cream dots.

I prefer mixing it further to *fully combine into a dough before freezing it in small chunks on a flat tray for 1 hour. Then, in the food processor, blitz the frozen chunks into a crumble. You can make more than you need and keep the crumble in a plastic container in the freezer for next time.*

As it is not baked at this stage, *you can make two or three times the amount needed for the recipe and keep the rest in the freezer, in a closed container, for next time.*

If using instant coffee, *there is no need to infuse the cream or re-weigh the cream.*

It is difficult to see when the cocoa crumble is baked *due to its colour, so make sure you are using a timer.*

lemon &
grapefruit
dacquoise

serves 8

PREPARATION TIME
1¼ hours (including the dacquoise base)

COOKING TIME
25 minutes (including the dacquoise base)

SPECIAL EQUIPMENT
2 piping bags, 12 mm (½ in) plain nozzle, 6 or 8mm (¼–⅜ in) plain nozzle, flat-based serving dish

PLANNING AHEAD
Bake the dacquoise meringue base.

There are quite a few techniques to get right when making this dessert, but it looks strikingly good when you present it to your guests.

INGREDIENTS

1 Dacquoise Meringue base
 (*see page 48*)

For the grapefruit jelly
1½ gelatine leaves
10 g (½ oz/2 teaspoons)
 potato flour (or you can
 use cornflour/cornstarch)
30 g (1 oz/2 tablespoons)
 caster (superfine) sugar
200 g (7 oz/ scant 1 cup)
 pink grapefruit
 juice

For the lemon cream
125 g (4½ oz) eggs
150 g (5½ oz/⅔ cup) caster
 (superfine) sugar
15 g (12 oz/1 tablespoon)
 yuzu juice (replace with
 lemon if you can't find yuzu)

zest of ⅔ lemon
130 g (4½ oz/generous
 ½ cup) lemon juice
40 g (1½ oz) unsalted butter
2 gelatine leaves, softened
 in cold water and drained

For the lemon mousse
125 g (4½ oz/½ cup)
 whipping cream
125 g (4½ oz/½ cup) lemon
 cream (see left)

To decorate
1 pink grapefruit, peeled and
 segmented

METHOD

MAKING THE GRAPEFRUIT JELLY

1. Soak the gelatine leaves in cold water for 10–15 minutes, then drain.
2. In a small cup, combine the potato flour and sugar with a quarter of the cold grapefruit juice.
3. Meanwhile, in a small saucepan, bring the remaining grapefruit juice to a quick boil. Stir the potato flour mixture with a small spoon to loosen, then quickly whisk it into the boiling grapefruit juice.
4. Bring it all back to the boil, whisking continuously for about 1 minute to thicken. Remove from the heat, add the drained gelatine leaves and transfer into a clean bowl to cool completely and thicken further.

PREPARING THE LEMON CREAM

5. In a medium bowl, whisk together the eggs, sugar, yuzu juice and lemon zest.
6. Meanwhile, in a medium saucepan, bring the lemon juice and butter to a quick boil. Whisk this into the egg mixture and, when fully combined, transfer it back into the pan and bring back to the boil for 20 seconds, whisking continuously.
7. Whisk in the drained gelatine leaves and transfer into a clean bowl set over a bowl of iced water to cool. After 15–20 minutes, when totally cold but before it sets too hard, remove the bowl of iced water.

MAKING THE LEMON MOUSSE

8. Whisk the cream until medium peaks form.
9. In another medium bowl, measure out 125 g (4½ oz) of the lemon cream. Knock it down with a whisk if slightly over-set, then fold in the whipped cream using the same whisk. Transfer to a piping bag with a large nozzle. The mixture should be of a pipeable texture. Reserve on the side or in the refrigerator for a few minutes.

ASSEMBLING THE DESSERT

10. Place the dacquoise meringue base on a serving dish (*see Chef's Touches*), then pour the thickened-but-not-quite-set grapefruit jelly into the lower centre part of the meringue (*see Chef's Touches*). Place in the refrigerator for 10–15 minutes to set the jelly.

11. Remove from the refrigerator and pipe on the lemon mousse, leaving a border of 2 cm (¾ in) around the edge of the meringue and mimicking the teardrop shape on the base, repeating and reducing with similar rows, until you reach the middle. Return to the refrigerator for a few minutes.

12. Meanwhile, knock the remaining lemon cream briefly with a whisk if it has over-set, then transfer it to another piping bag with a medium plain nozzle. Pipe a few large drops of cream in the gaps between the lemon mousse, as per the photo. Finish by elegantly placing the grapefruit segments on top of the dessert. Reserve in the refrigerator until required.

───────────────(CHEF'S TOUCHES)───────────────

If you want to make this dessert *the day before or keep it a bit longer and prevent it from getting too soft, brush the centre of the meringue with a thin coat of lukewarm melted white chocolate to create a waterproof membrane. Allow to set*

completely in the refrigerator before pouring over the jelly.

If the grapefruit jelly is too liquid, *it softens the meringue and makes it fragile, so it will not have any texture.*

If your heart is not in it or you're pushed for time, *you can simplify the recipe by using the dacquoise base and filling it up with Chantilly cream and fresh seasonal berries.*

orange savarin

with Grand Marnier diplomat cream

serves 8–10

This savarin has the typical loop shape, using a brioche-like dough that, once baked, is soaked in a light sugar syrup and glazed. Here, I combine cinnamon, vanilla and star anise with orange juice, and it is served with a light cream and plenty of citrus segments. It is a great-looking dish in the winter, when citrus fruits are at their best.

PREPARATION TIME
1 hour, plus 1¾ hours proving

COOKING TIME
40 minutes

SPECIAL EQUIPMENT
Mixer with paddle attachment, 20 cm (8 in) non-stick savarin mould, piping bag and large plain nozzle, temperature probe, deep 24 cm (9½ in) square baking tray or similar to accommodate the mould later on

PLANNING AHEAD
Make the pastry cream in advance.

INGREDIENTS

For the savarin dough
200 g (7 oz/1⅓ cups) strong bread flour
50 g (1¾ oz/3½ tablespoons) lukewarm whole milk
15 g (½ oz/2 teaspoons) fresh yeast
4 g (¼ oz/1 teaspoon) salt
20 g (¾ oz/1½ tablespoons) caster (superfine) sugar
2 large eggs
85 g (3 oz) unsalted butter, softened, plus extra melted butter for greasing

For the soaking syrup
700 g (1 lb 9 oz/scant 3 cups) orange juice
300 g (10½ oz/1⅓ cups) caster (superfine) sugar
1 cinnamon stick
½ vanilla pod, split lengthways and seeds scraped out

2 star anise
Grand Marnier or Cointreau liqueur, to taste

For the diplomat cream
200 g (7 oz/scant 1 cup) whipping cream
20 g (¾ oz/1½ tablespoons) icing (powdered) sugar
200 g (7 oz) Pastry Cream (*see page 54*)
1 gelatine leaf, soaked and drained
2 dashes of Grand Marnier

For the glaze and the garnish
5 citrus fruits, including blood oranges when in season and pink grapefruit
100 g (3½ oz) clear apricot jelly or jam
50 g (1¾ oz) good-quality citrus marmalade, melted

See image on page 237

MAKING THE DOUGH

1. In the mixer bowl, whisk together by hand 30 g (1 oz/¼ cup) of the flour with the lukewarm milk (see Chef's Touches) and the yeast. Allow to prove in a warm place for about 30 minutes, or until it has doubled in volume. Add the remaining flour, along with the salt, sugar and eggs and, using the paddle attachment, combine on a low speed for 2–3 minutes to form a dough. Increase to medium speed for 10–12 minutes. Add the soft butter and combine on a low–medium speed for 2–3 minutes, or until the butter is fully incorporated. Leave the dough in the bowl to prove for about 45 minutes.

2. Meanwhile, brush the inside of the savarin mould with a thin coat of melted butter and reserve on the side. Transfer the dough into a piping bag fitted with a large plain nozzle and pipe 300–350 g (10½–12 oz) of dough evenly into the prepared mould (see Chef's Touches).

3. Allow to prove for about 30 minutes on the side or until it reaches two-thirds of the way up the mould. Preheat the oven to 170°C fan (340°F).

4. Bake for about 30 minutes. Using oven gloves or a thick, dry cloth, flip the savarin quickly out of the mould and return it to the oven on a rack to dry off for a further 10–12 minutes. It should be evenly baked all over. Remove from the oven and allow to cool completely.

SOAKING THE SAVARIN

5. In a medium saucepan, bring the orange juice and sugar to a quick boil, then add the cinnamon, vanilla pod and star anise. Turn off the heat and leave to infuse for 30 minutes, then remove all the spices and add the liqueur to taste.

6. When completely cold, use a toothpick to prick plenty of little holes all over the flat base of the savarin to allow the syrup to go through later on. Place the savarin mould on a deep baking tray. Warm up the soaking syrup to 60°C (140°F) and pour about a quarter of it inside the savarin mould.

Place the baked savarin back inside the mould, on top of the syrup, to soak while holding its shape. Using a ladle, pour about half the remaining warm syrup all over the back of the savarin and quickly stretch a piece of cling film (plastic wrap) over the whole tray. Leave to steam and soak for about 10 minutes. Peel off the cling film, empty any syrup from the tray back into the pan, then reheat the syrup to 60°C (140°F), and repeat the soaking process until it has been completely absorbed. Allow to cool completely.

PREPARING THE DIPLOMAT CREAM AND THE GARNISHES

6. Whip the whipping cream and icing sugar to firm peaks. Set aside. Whisk the pastry cream until smooth, then warm it through in a pan over a low heat or in the microwave until it reaches 40–45°C (104–133°F). Add the gelatine leaf and melt and combine, then transfer to a medium bowl to cool.

7. Once cool, whisk the pastry cream again until smooth and add the Grand Marnier. Now fold in the whipped cream mixture with the whisk and set aside.

9. Meanwhile, using a paring knife, peel the citrus fruits and release the segments. Place into a colander to drain off the excess juice.

SERVING

10. Flip the soaked savarin (still in the mould) over a cooling rack sitting over a deep baking tray and leave for 5 minutes to drain any excess soaking juices. Carefully slide the savarin off the cooling rack, with the mould still on, then transfer to a large circular serving dish and take the mould away.

11. In a small pan over a low heat, melt the apricot jelly, then brush it all over the rounded side of the savarin. With a rubber spatula, fill up the centre hole of the savarin with the diplomat cream. Level nicely with the spatula.

12. In a large bowl, combine the melted marmalade with the citrus segments. Arrange them harmoniously on top of the diplomat cream before serving.

Make sure the milk is lukewarm and not hotter than 40°C (104°F), as the heat will kill the yeast and it will not work.

The recipe makes a little bit more dough than needed for a 20 cm (8 in) savarin mould, but you can pipe the spare dough into 30 g (1 oz) portions in a muffin tray to make individual ones. Bake for about 30 minutes at 175°C (345°F).

juju's 'ultra' chocolate sponge cake

I made this cake for my daughter's 21st birthday when we were in lockdown, as she wanted a rich chocolate cake. As she usually prefers milk chocolate, I made the recipe using both dark and milk chocolate, with a bit of raspberry compote to cut through the richness. This cake tastes best served on the day it's made and at room temperature.

serves 10—12

PREPARATION TIME
40 minutes, plus 1 hour 10 minutes setting

COOKING TIME
50–55 minutes, plus 2 hours cooling

SPECIAL EQUIPMENT
18 cm (7 in) cake ring, 6 cm (2½ in) deep, mixer with whisk attachment, flat serving dish, piping bag, 8 mm (⅜ in) plain nozzle, 20 cm (8 in) cake card or similar, blowtorch

PLANNING AHEAD
Plan to bake your sponge at least a couple of hours before building your cake, or even the day before, as it has a fragile texture and it will be easier to slice when completely cold. Make a batch of milk chocolate curls the day before and keep them in a box in a cool place or in the refrigerator.

CHEF'S TOUCHES

Prick the cake in the centre with a paring knife – *if it comes out clean, the cake is baked.*

Do not place the ganache in the fridge, *or it will go too hard.*

INGREDIENTS

For the chocolate sponge
100 g (3½ oz) unsalted butter, softened, plus extra for greasing
225 g (8 oz/1¾ cups) plain (all-purpose) flour
20 g (¾ oz/1½ tablespoons) cocoa powder
4 g (¼ oz/1 teaspoon) baking powder
5 g (¼ oz 1 teaspoon) bicarbonate of soda (baking soda)
25 g (1 oz/scant 2 tablespoons) vegetable oil
225 g (8 oz/1 cup) caster (superfine) sugar
250 g (9 oz/1 cup) whole milk

For the chocolate ganache
165 g (5¾ oz) good-quality dark chocolate (65% cocoa or more)
165 g (5¾ oz) good-quality milk chocolate (not too sweet; 35–40% cocoa is ideal)

200 g (7 oz/scant 1 cup) whipping cream
70 g (2½ oz) unsalted butter, diced
80 g (2¾ oz) honey

For the raspberry compote
120 g (4¼ oz) fresh raspberries
30 g (1 oz/2 tablespoons) caster (superfine) sugar
dash of lemon juice

For the chocolate drip glaze
60 g (2 oz/¼ cup) whipping cream
40 g (1½ oz) dark chocolate, chopped into small pieces

To decorate
1 batch of milk or dark Chocolate Curls (*see page 64*)
10 g (½ oz/2 teaspoons) cocoa powder
10 g (½ oz/2 teaspoons) icing (powdered) sugar
Edible gold leaf (optional)

See method overleaf

BAKING THE SPONGE

1. Preheat the oven to 170°C fan (340°F). Grease the inside of the 18 cm (7 in) cake ring with a little bit of butter, then stick a band of baking parchment, the same height as the ring, all the way around. On a flat baking tray, place the lined ring on a slightly bigger square of baking parchment, sitting on top of a slightly larger square of foil. Roll the foil and paper towards the ring to create a tight seal and prevent the mixture running away when baking.

2. In a medium bowl, sift together the flour, cocoa powder, baking powder and bicarbonate of soda. In the mixer with the whisk attachment, cream together the butter, oil and sugar. Gradually add the milk, followed by the dry ingredients. Using a rubber spatula, pour the batter into the prepared cake ring and bake for 50–55 minutes (*see Chef's Touches*). Remove from the oven and slide the cake onto a cooling rack. Remove the ring and leave for at least a couple of hours to cool completely.

MAKING THE CHOCOLATE GANACHE

3. In a medium bowl, combine all the chocolate and partially melt over a hot bain-marie or in the microwave for 40 seconds.

4. Meanwhile, in a small saucepan, bring the whipping cream to a quick boil, then pour it over the chocolate. Using a hand whisk, combine the cream and the chocolate, then add the butter. When it's fully incorporated, add the honey. Cover the ganache with cling film (plastic wrap) and reserve on the side, in a cool place, to set for about an hour (*see Chef's Touches*).

MAKING THE RASPBERRY COMPÔTE

5. In a small saucepan, bring all the ingredients to the boil for a couple of minutes to break down the raspberries into a syrupy texture. Set aside.

BUILDING THE CAKE

6. Using a serrated knife, slice the sponge horizontally into three equal slices. Keep them on top of each other for now. Place the cleaned baking ring you used for baking the sponge on a cake card or a flat tray lined with baking parchment.

7. Carefully pick up one layer of sponge and place inside the ring. Using the piping bag and the 8 mm (⅜ in) plain nozzle, pipe a small amount of partially set ganache between the sponge and the ring to fill up the gap all around. Pipe a bit more ganache around the ring and, using a small palette knife or the back of a spoon, spread it to cover the inside of the ring completely to create a nice smooth wall that will help when de-moulding the cake later on.

8. With a spoon, spread half the raspberry compôte all over the sponge in the ring, then pipe a disc of ganache all over the top. Place another layer of sponge on top, pressing down gently, and repeat with another layer of the compôte and the ganache. Finally, place the last slice on top and cap the ring with the remaining ganache, levelling neatly with a large palette knife. Place the cake in the refrigerator to set for about 1 hour.

FINISHING THE CAKE

9. Remove the cake from the refrigerator and place it on a flat presentation dish. Using a blowtorch, carefully warm the ring all around, just enough to slide it upwards and remove it. Place the cake back in the refrigerator for 10 minutes to set the sides.

10. Meanwhile, prepare the drip glaze. In a small pan, heat the cream to a simmer and pour it over the chopped chocolate in a bowl. Leave for 1 minute to melt the chocolate, then whisk together until smooth.

11. Remove the cake from the refrigerator and, using a large spoon, create the chocolate dripping effect all around the edge of the cake by slowly pouring over the chocolate drip glaze.

12. Arrange the large chocolate curls on top, placing them randomly and elegantly. Using a small sieve, dust the cocoa powder and icing sugar all over the top. For the final touch and if you can find any, finish with half a leaf of edible gold leaf — just because we can.

pineapple baked floating island

with piña colada sauce

This floating island is baked in the oven and served with fresh pineapple that cuts through the sweetness of the caramel to bring some freshness to the dish.

◆◆◆ ────────────

serves 6

PREPARATION TIME
30 minutes

COOKING TIME
25 minutes, plus 30 minutes cooling

SPECIAL EQUIPMENT
20–22 cm (8–8½ in) non-stick savarin mould, jug blender, temperature probe. If you have an old balloon whisk, you can cut the rounded part with pliers to create a broom-like handle.

PLANNING AHEAD
Bake the meringue a couple of hours before serving to allow it to cool and de-mould easily. You can also make the piña colada sauce a few hours in advance and keep it in the refrigerator until serving.

INGREDIENTS

For the piña colada sauce
240 g (8½ oz/¼) fresh pineapple, peeled and chopped
75 g (2 ½ oz/5 tablespoons) unsweetened coconut milk
2 egg yolks (50 g/2 oz)
20 g (¾ oz/1½ tablespoons) caster (superfine) sugar
1 gelatine leaf, soaked in cold water and drained
10 ml (2 teaspoons) Malibu
10 ml (2 teaspoons) white rum

For the baked poached meringue
170 g (6 oz) egg whites
140 g (5 oz/⅔ cup) caster (superfine) sugar
1 vanilla pod

To decorate
¾ fresh pineapple, peeled
50 g (1¾ oz) apricot jam, melted
zest of ½ lime
a few fresh mint leaves, finely chopped, plus extra (optional) to serve
edible flowers, to serve

For the caramel filé
40 ml (scant 3 tablespoon) cold water
150 g (5½ oz/⅔ cup) caster (superfine) sugar
1 teaspoon glucose syrup

METHOD

MAKING THE PIÑA COLADA SAUCE

1. With a jug blender, blitz the fresh chopped pineapple into a smooth purée. Place it in a small saucepan and whisk in the remaining ingredients, except the gelatine leaf and alcohol, until fully combined. Cook over a medium heat, mixing continuously with a rubber spatula, until it reaches 90°C (194°F). Drain the gelatine leaf and dissolve it into the hot purée. Transfer straight away into a clean bowl sitting on ice (this will stop the cooking). Leave it to cool completely, then add the Malibu and white rum. Reserve in the refrigerator.

MAKING THE BAKED POACHED MERINGUE

2. Preheat the oven to 150°C (300°F).

3. Place the egg white and sugar in the mixer bowl. Split the vanilla pod in half, scrape out the seeds and add them to the egg whites and sugar. Start whisking the meringue on a fast speed until it forms medium to firm peaks.

4. Using a large spoon, line the savarin mould with a quarter of the meringue, applying gentle pressure to remove any air pockets and obtain a smooth finish. With a rubber spatula, transfer the rest of the meringue on top and level. Clean the edges, passing your finger around the mould. Place the mould into a slightly larger ovenproof sauté pan or a deep baking tray. Pour some hot water into the pan or tray around the mould; it should come up to half the height of the meringue. Bake for 20–25 minutes. Prick a knife blade into the meringue; if it comes out clean, it is baked. Take the pan out of the oven and carefully remove the meringue mould from the hot water. Leave to rest and cool on a rack for 5–10 minutes. Using a dry cloth, grab the savarin mould and carefully flip the meringue out onto the serving dish. If the meringue sticks, allow it a bit of time to come down slowly. Set aside (*see Chef's Touches*).

Method continued overleaf

PREPARING THE FRUIT GARNISH

5. Peel and cut the fresh pineapple into small chunks and combine it with the melted apricot jam. Add the lime zest and mint leaves.

MAKING THE CARAMEL FILÉ

6. Prepare your equipment first. Prepare a large baking tray or line the table with baking parchment. On the side, have a couple of forks ready or a cut/trimmed old balloon whisk.

7. Pour the cold water into a small pan, then add the sugar and glucose syrup. Heat over a medium heat, cook it until it has reached a golden caramel colour (*see Chef's Touches*). Stop the cooking of the caramel by quickly dipping the base of the pan into a bowl of cold water for 30 seconds.

8. Remove the pan from the bowl and place it safely next to the baking tray on a heatproof mat. When the caramel thickens, but remains pliable, dip the ends of the cut whisk or forks into the caramel. Pull them out carefully, stretching the caramel into thin strings, and move your hand quickly back and forth, about 20 cm (8 in) above the baking tray to allow the caramel to cool and create the thin filé texture. Repeat several times until you create enough volume to make a crown the size of the top of the meringue. Reserve on the side if you'll be using it soon, or placed in a dry, airtight box lined with baking parchment to keep it for a couple of hours. Keep the rest of the caramel in the pan to pour over the meringue.

TO SERVE

9. Get the meringue loop ready near you. Over a low heat, melt the leftover caramel from the filé. Pour a little all over the top of the meringue and let it drip down the sides. Fill the centre of the meringue loop with the pineapple and mint garnish, and pour some of the piña colada sauce around the meringue. Keep the rest of the sauce in a jug or sauce boat to add when serving. Place the crown of caramel filé on top. Decorate with a few small mint leaves or small edible flower petals.

CHEF'S TOUCHES

The meringue *may release some water that will need to be drained before finishing and serving the dessert.*

Instead of making the piña colada sauce, *you can make a fresh pineapple coulis if that is easier. Also, you can use the same method but use raspberry coulis instead and serve with fresh raspberries.*

For the caramel filé, *it's better to have a light golden colour rather than brown, in order for it to be more resistant to humidity and last longer.*

Instead of a balloon whisk, *you can use a couple of forks and held together back-to-back.*

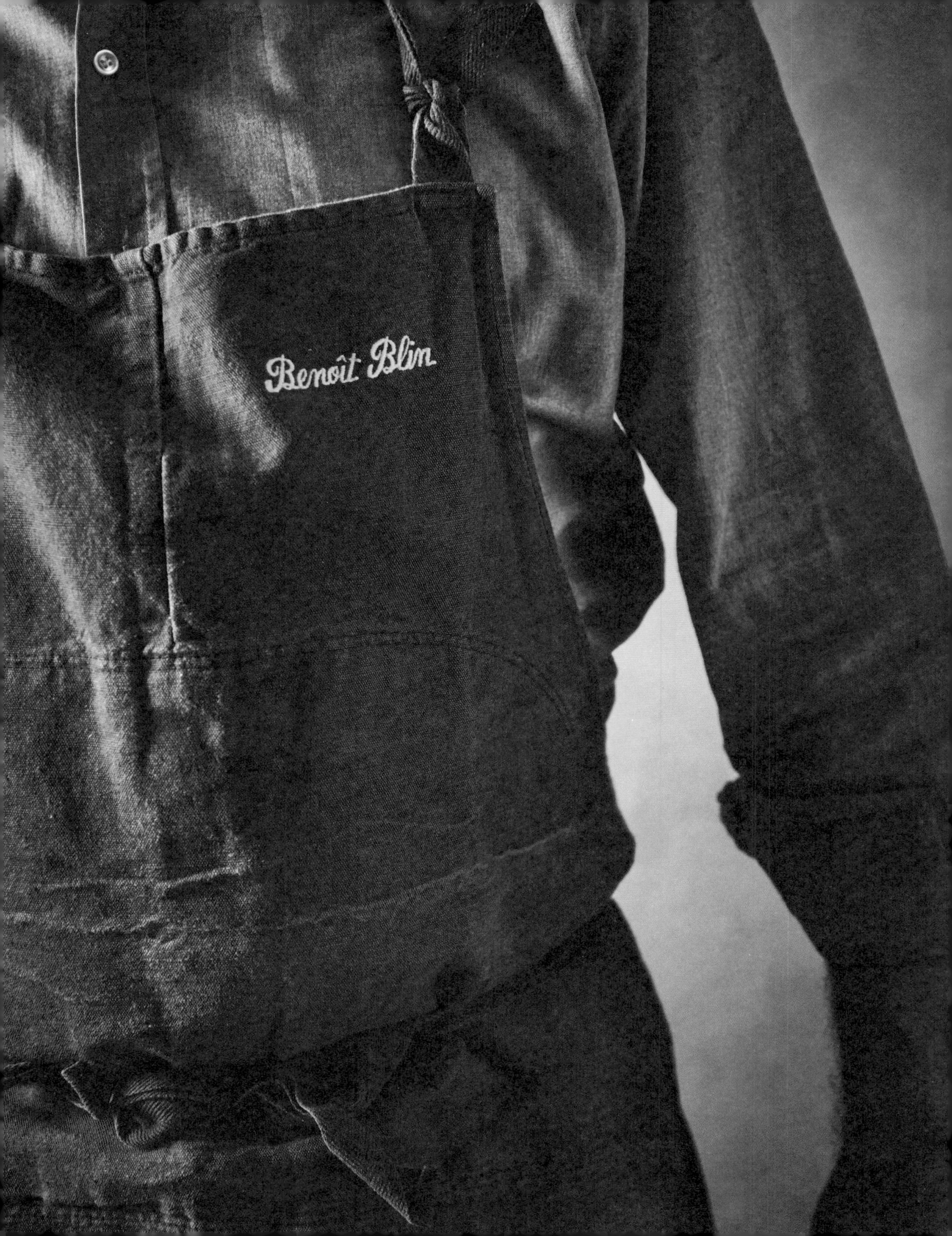
Benoît Blin

index

Page numbers in *italic* refer to the photographs

A

almonds
  almond cream 56
  almond croissants *100*, 101, *102–3*
  chocolate fondant 184–5, *185*
  dacquoise meringue 48, *49–51*
  macarons 214–15, *215*
  Opéra petit gâteau 221–3, *222*
  pear almondine tarte 146, *147*
  raspberry financiers 160, *161*
  strawberry financier 200–3, *201–2*
amaretto & chocolate cream 184–5
apples
  apple compôte 61
  apple kouign-amann 120–1, *121*
  my apple pie 126–7, *127–9*
  tarte Tatin 138–41, *139–41*
apricot jelly
  lime rum glaze 165
apricot tarte boulangère 124, *125*

B

banana & rum cake 165
biscuit cuillère sponge 44, *45–7*
  blackcurrant charlotte 190–3, *191–3*
  coffee & cardamom tiramisu 194–7, *195–6*
biscuits
  crack-cao biscuits 76, *77*
  triple chocolate chip American-style cookies 78, 79
  see also shortbread
blackberries
  summer berry Jésuites 212–13, *213*
blackcurrant charlotte 44, 190–3, *191–3*
blind-baking pastry 24, 28
blueberries
  blueberry & kirsch tartlets 210–11, *211*
  blueberry muffins 152, *153*
  summer berry Jésuites 212–13, *213*
  summer berry Victoria sponge 172, *173*
brioche
  brioche crème 107, 109, *110–11*
  brioche dough 42, *43*
  brioche loaf 104, *105*
  candied fruit brioche 112, *113*
  little brioche rolls *106*, 108
  polonaise brioche 216, *217*
Brittany shortbreads 84, *85*
buns, Chelsea 116, *117–19*
butter 16
  croissant dough 39, *40–1*
  quick puff pastry 30, *31–3*
  spiced butter 116
buttercream 58
  coffee buttercream 221
butterscotch sauce, lemon 63

C

cakes
  banana & rum cake 165
  double chocolate & vanilla marble cake 156, 157
  Juju's 'ultra' chocolate sponge cake 240–3, *241–2*
  madeleines 158, *159*
  muscovado & dark rum fruit cake 154–5, *155*
  my gluten-free lemon drizzle cake 166, *167*
  raspberry financiers 160, *161*
  yoghurt cake 168, *169*
candied fruit
  candied fruit brioche 112, *113*
  polonaise brioche 216, *217*
caramel
  caramel filé 244–6
  caramelised hazelnuts 230–3
  coffee & orange crème brûlée *178*, 179
  hazelnut praline paste 186–7, *187–9*
  lemon butterscotch sauce 63
  millionaire's chocolate tart 132, *133*
  tarte Tatin 138–41, *139–41*
  vanilla crème caramel 176, *177*
cardamom pods
  coffee & cardamom tiramisu 194–7, *195–6*
Chantilly cream 59
  chocolate & vanilla profiteroles 198–9, *199*
  coffee Chantilly cream 230–3
charlotte
  biscuit cuillère sponge for 44
  blackcurrant charlotte 44, 190–3, *191–3*

Chelsea buns 116, *117–19*
cherries (glacé)
    muscovado & dark rum fruit cake 154–5, *155*
chocolate 16
    amaretto & chocolate cream 184–5
    chocolate & pistachio pain Swiss 96, *97–9*
    chocolate & vanilla profiteroles 198–9, *199*
    chocolate coins & discs 64, *68–9*
    chocolate cream 132, 230–3
    chocolate crumble 230–3, *231–2*
    chocolate curls 64, *66–7*
    chocolate drip glaze 240–3
    chocolate fondant 184–5, *185*
    chocolate ganache 221, 240–3
    chocolate glaze 156, 221
    chocolate scones 164
    coffee & cardamom tiramisu 194–7, *195–6*
    crack-cao biscuits 76, 77
    dark chocolate ganache filling 214
    double chocolate & vanilla marble cake 156, *157*
    hot chocolate sauce 60
    Juju's 'ultra' chocolate sponge cake 240–3, *241–2*
    macarons 214–15, *215*
    millionaire's chocolate tart 132, *133*
    techniques 64, *65–9*
    tempering 64
    triple chocolate chip American-style cookies 78, *79*
choux pastry 34, *35–7*
    chocolate & vanilla profiteroles 198–9, *199*
    coffee éclairs 218–20, *219–20*
    hazelnut Paris-Brest 186–7, *187–9*
coconut cream 226–9
coconut milk
    piña colada sauce 244
coffee
    coffee & cardamom tiramisu 194–7, *195–6*
    coffee & orange crème brûlée *178*, 179
    coffee buttercream 221
    coffee Chantilly cream 230–3
    coffee éclairs 218–20, *219–20*
    coffee extract 71
    Opéra petit gâteau 221–3, *222*
compôte
    apple compôte 61

fruit compôte 200–3
cookies *see* biscuits
crack-cao biscuits 76, *77*
cranberries (dried)
    muscovado & dark rum fruit cake 154–5, *155*
craquelin, vanilla 34
cream
    almond cream 56
    amaretto & chocolate cream 184–5
    blackcurrant charlotte 190–3, *191–3*
    Chantilly cream 59
    chocolate cream 132, 230–3
    chocolate ganache 221, 240–3
    coconut cream 226–9
    coffee & cardamom tiramisu 194–7, *195–6*
    coffee Chantilly cream 230–3
    custard tart 144, *145*
    dark chocolate ganache filling 214
    diplomat cream 238–9
    lemon butterscotch sauce 63
    lime & tonka mascarpone cream 200–3, *201–2*
    pastry cream 54, *55*
    soft caramel 132, *133*
crème anglaise, vanilla 57
crème brûlée, coffee & orange *178*, 179
crème caramel, vanilla 176, *177*
crêpes
    crêpes Suzette 174, *175*
    French crêpes 52
croissant dough 39, *40–1*
    almond croissants *100*, 101, *102–3*
    chocolate & pistachio pain Swiss 96, *97–9*
    croissants 90, *91–3*
    pain aux raisins 94, *95*
crumble, chocolate 230–3, 231–2
custard
    custard tart 144, *145*
    rhubarb & custard tart 130, *131*

D
dacquoise meringue 48, *49–51*
    lemon & grapefruit dacquoise 234–5, *236*
decorations
    caramel filé 244–6

chocolate coins & discs 64, *68—9*

chocolate curls 64, *66—7*

desserts 171—207

blackcurrant charlotte 190-3, *191-3*

chocolate & vanilla profiteroles 198-9, *199*

chocolate fondant 184-5, *185*

coffee & cardamom tiramisu 194-7, *195-6*

coffee & orange crème brûlée *178*, 179

crêpes Suzette 174, *175*

hazelnut Paris-Brest 186-7, *187-9*

hot soufflés 204-5, *205-7*

{le }riz au lait 182, *183*

strawberry financier 200-3, *201-2*

summer berry Victoria sponge 172, 173

vanilla crème caramel 176, 177

waffles 180, 181

diplomat cream 212—13, 238—9

double chocolate & vanilla marble cake 156, *157*

doughnuts, passion fruit 114, *115*

E

éclairs, coffee 218—20, *219—20*

eggs 16

egg wash 70

equipment 18—19

F

figs (dried)

muscovado & dark rum fruit cake 154—5, *155*

financiers

raspberry financiers 160, *161*

strawberry financier 200—3, *201—2*

flan vanille *148*, 149

floating island, pineapple baked 244—6, *245*

flour 16

French crêpes 52

fruit cake, muscovado & dark rum 154—5, *155*

G

ganache, chocolate 214, 221, 240—3

gâteau Basque 134—6, *135*

glazes 218

blackcurrant glaze 190—3, *191—3*

blueberry glaze 210

chocolate drip glaze 240

chocolate glaze 156, 221

egg wash 70

lime rum glaze 165

orange glaze 238

golden raisins *see* sultanas

Grand Marnier

crêpes Suzette 174, *175*

hot soufflés 204—5, *205—7*

grapefruit

lemon & grapefruit dacquoise 234—5, *236*

H

hazelnuts

caramelised hazelnuts 230—3

hazelnut Paris-Brest 186—7, *187—9*

hot chocolate sauce 60

I

ice cream

chocolate & vanilla profiteroles 198—9, *199*

icing 212

almond croissants *100*, 101, *102—3*

ingredients 16

J

jelly, grapefruit 234

Jésuites, summer berry 212—13, *213*

Juju's 'ultra' chocolate sponge cake 240—3, *241—2*

K

kirsch eau de vie

blueberry & kirsch tartlets 210—11, *211*

diplomat cream 212—13

pistachio paste 60

polonaise brioche 216, *217*

kiwi fruit

pavlova 226—9, *227—8*

kouign-amann, apple 120—1, *121*

L

laminating croissant dough 39, *40—1*

lemon
    lemon & grapefruit dacquoise 234–5, *236*
    lemon butterscotch sauce 63
    my gluten-free lemon drizzle cake 166, *167*
limes
    lime & tonka mascarpone cream 200–3, *201–2*
    lime rum glaze 165
lining a tart case 24, 28
liquorice
    macarons 214–15, *215*

M

macarons 214–15, *215*
madeleines 158, *159*
Malibu
    piña colada sauce 244
mangoes
    passion fruit curd 114
    pavlova 226–9, *227–8*
marble cake, double chocolate & vanilla 156, *157*
marzipan
    almond croissants *100*, 101, *102–3*
mascarpone
    coffee & cardamom tiramisu 194–7, *195–6*
    lime & tonka mascarpone cream 200–3, *201–2*
meringue
    dacquoise meringue 48, *49–51*
    lemon & grapefruit dacquoise 234–5, *236*
    pavlova 226–9, *227–8*
    pineapple baked floating island 244–6, *245*
    polonaise brioche 216, *217*
milk 16
    flan vanille *148*, 149
    pastry cream 54, *55*
    le riz au lait 182, *183*
    vanilla crème anglaise 57
    vanilla crème caramel 176, *177*
millionaire's chocolate tart 132, *133*
muffins, blueberry 152, *153*
muscovado & dark rum fruit cake 154–5, *155*
my apple pie 126–7, *127–9*
my gluten-free lemon drizzle cake 166, *167*

O

Opéra petit gâteau 221–3, *222*
oranges
    coffee & orange crème brûlée *178*, 179
    crêpes Suzette 174, *175*
    orange savarin *237*, 238–9

P

pain aux raisins 94, *95*
palmiers 86, *87*
pancakes
    crêpes Suzette 174, *175*
    French crêpes 52
Paris-Brest, hazelnut 186–7, *187–9*
passion fruit
    passion fruit doughnuts 114, *115*
    pavlova 226–9, *227–8*
pastries
    almond croissants *100*, 101, *102–3*
    chocolate & pistachio pain Swiss 96, *97–9*
    chocolate & vanilla profiteroles 198–9, *199*
    coffee éclairs 218–20, *219–20*
    croissants 90, *91–3*
    pain aux raisins 94, *95*
    palmiers 86, *87*
    summer berry Jésuites 212–13, *213*
pastry
    blind-baking 24, 28
    choux pastry 34, *35–7*
    lining a tart case 24, 28
    quick puff pastry 30, *31–3*
    sablé pastry tart case 24, *25–7*
    shortcrust pastry tart case 28, *29*
pastry cream 54, *55*
    apricot tarte boulangère 124, *125*
    blueberry & kirsch tartlets 210–11, *211*
    brioche crème *107*, 109, *110–11*
    candied fruit brioche 112, *113*
    chocolate & pistachio pain Swiss 96, *97–9*
    coffee éclairs 218–20, *219–20*
    diplomat cream 212–13, 238–9
    gâteau Basque 134–6, *135*
    hazelnut Paris-Brest 186–7, *187–9*

hot soufflés 204—5, *205—7*
pain aux raisins 94, *95*
polonaise brioche 216, *217*
pavlova 226—9, *227—8*
pear almondine tarte 146, *147*
pecan nuts
    crack-cao biscuits 76, *77*
pies
    gâteau Basque 134—6, *135*
    my apple pie 126—7, *127—9*
    see also tarts
piña colada sauce 244
pineapple baked floating island 244—6, *245*
piping
    biscuit cuillère sponge 44, *47*
    dacquoise meringue 48, *50—1*
pistachios
    chocolate & pistachio pain Swiss 96, *97—9*
    chocolate fondant 184—5, *185*
    crack-cao biscuits 76, *77*
    hot soufflés 204—5, *205—7*
    pistachio paste 60
    pistachio sauce 184—5
    strawberry & pistachio tart *142*, 143
polonaise brioche 216, *217*
praline paste, hazelnut 186—7, *187—9*
profiteroles, chocolate & vanilla 198—9, *199*
prunes
    gâteau Basque 134—6, *135*
puff pastry 30, *31—3*
    apricot tarte boulangère *124*, *125*
    flan vanille *148*, 149
    palmiers 86, *87*
    summer berry Jésuites 212—13, *213*
    tarte Tatin 138—41, *139—41*

R
raisins
    pain aux raisins 94, *95*
raspberries
    hot soufflés 204—5, *205—7*
    raspberry compôte 240—3
    raspberry financiers 160, *161*
    strawberry financier 200—3, *201—2*

summer berry Jésuites 212—13, *213*
summer berry Victoria sponge 172, *173*
redcurrants
    summer berry Victoria sponge 172, *173*
rhubarb & custard tart 130
rice
    le riz au lait 182, *183*
rolls, little brioche *106*, 108
rum
    almond cream 56
    banana & rum cake 165
    French crêpes 52
    lime rum glaze 165
    muscovado & dark rum fruit cake 154—5, *155*

S
sablé pastry 24, *25—7*
    blueberry & kirsch tartlets 210—11, *211*
    custard tart 144, *145*
    millionaire's chocolate tart 132, *133*
    pear almondine tarte 146, *147*
    strawberry & pistachio tart *142*, 143
sauces
    hot chocolate sauce 60
    lemon butterscotch sauce 63
    orange and butter sauce 174
    piña colada sauce 244
    pistachio sauce 184—5
    vanilla crème anglaise 57
savarin, orange *237*, 238—9
scones *162*, 163
    chocolate scones 164
shortbread
    Brittany shortbreads 84, *85*
    vanilla diamond shortbreads *80*, 81, *82—3*
    see also biscuits
shortcrust pastry 28, *29*
    rhubarb & custard tart 130, *131*
soufflés, hot 204—5, *205—7*
spiced butter 116
sponge
    biscuit cuillère sponge 44, *45—7*
    Juju's 'ultra' chocolate sponge cake 240—3, *241—2*
    summer berry Victoria sponge 172, *173*

Victoria sponge 53

strawberries
strawberry & pistachio tart *142*, 143
strawberry financier 200–3, *201–2*
summer berry Jésuites 212–13, *213*
summer berry Victoria sponge 172, *173*

sugar syrup 70
sultanas (golden raisins) *162*, 163
Chelsea buns 116, *117–19*
muscovado & dark rum fruit cake 154–5, *155*
pain aux raisins 94, *95*
summer berry Jésuites 212–13, *213*
summer berry Victoria sponge 172, *173*
Swiss meringue 216
syrup, sugar 70

T

tarts
apricot tarte boulangère 124, *125*
blueberry & kirsch tartlets 210–11, *211*
custard tart 144, *145*
flan vanille *148*, 149
millionaire's chocolate tart 132, *133*
pear almondine tarte 146, *147*
rhubarb & custard tart 130, *131*
sablé pastry tart case 24, *25–7*
shortcrust pastry tart case 28, *29*
strawberry & pistachio tart *142*, 143
tarte Tatin 138–41, *139–41*
tempering chocolate 64
tiramisu
biscuit cuillère sponge for 44
coffee & cardamom tiramisu 194–7, *195–6*
tonka beans
lime & tonka mascarpone cream 200–3, *201–2*
triple chocolate chip American-style cookies 78, *79*

V

vanilla
chocolate & vanilla profiteroles 198–9, *199*
double chocolate & vanilla marble cake 156, *157*
flan vanille *148*, 149
hot soufflés 204–5, *205–7*
lime & tonka mascarpone cream 200–3, *201–2*

pastry cream 54, *55*
le riz au lait 182, *183*
vanilla craquelin 34
vanilla crème anglaise 57
vanilla crème caramel 176, *177*
vanilla diamond shortbreads 80, 81, *82–3*
Victoria sponge 53
summer berry Victoria sponge 172, *173*
Viennoiseries 89–121
almond croissants *100*, 101, *102–3*
apple kouign-amann 120–1, *121*
brioche crème *107*, 109, *110–11*
brioche loaf 104, *105*
candied fruit brioche 112, *113*
Chelsea buns 116, *117–19*
chocolate & pistachio pain Swiss 96, *97–9*
croissants 90, *91–3*
little brioche rolls *106*, 108
pain aux raisins 94, *95*
passion fruit doughnuts 114, *115*

W

waffles 180, *181*

Y

yeast 16
apple kouign-amann 120–1, *121*
brioche dough 42, *43*
Chelsea buns 116, *117–19*
croissant dough 39, *40–1*
orange savarin *237*, 238–9
passion fruit doughnuts 114, *115*
yoghurt cake 168, *169*

thanks

Creating a book without support, like most things in life, would not be possible. Therefore, my immense gratitude goes to, in no particular order:

My Publisher Hardie Grant and the whole team lead by Isabel Gonzalez-Prendergast – thank you for trusting me and guiding me throughout the laborious yet rewarding & enjoyable process of making my first book, with Sam Folan our photographer & Gizem Kumbaraci his assistant, Lizzie Kamenetzky our food stylist & Georgia Rudd her assistant, Jen Kay our prop stylist and Nikki Dupin our designer.

My Agent, Rosemary Scoular, for helping me find the best publisher to create this book.

Raymond Blanc, RB. Who, without hesitation, supported me with this project and from day one showed enthusiasm and mentorship. A special thanks for the lovely and personal intro for the book.

The Belmond and Le Manoir team – the company I work for, who have given me support and resources for this book to come together, with a special thanks to Adam,

RB's right-hand man, for all his advice using his wealth of experience in making books for RB. To the cookery school team for the use of their facilities and to Niall Kingston, our general manager.

Le Manoir Pastry team – Glen, Matt, Francesca, Nick, Camilla, Emma M, Emma P, Katie, Max, Melanie, Josh, Dan, Monica, Brook, Mirabelle – for their patience and hard work throughout the year.

My family, with all my profound affection. My wife Sophie, my daughter Justine, my son Francois and my Maman Denise. For being my biggest supporters, a big source of inspiration and for their love and motivation.

To my former Chef Pâtissier when I was working at the Ritz in Paris and good friend Christian Forais, for helping me and encouraging me when I was a young chef and for perfecting my skills under his supervision

To Kenwood UK and Nadia Hobbs for supporting me, having used their mixer to work out all the recipes in this book.

Benoit Blin has been Raymond Blanc's Head Pastry Chef at the award-winning Le Manoir aux Quat'Saisons in Oxfordshire since 1995. A judge and host on Channel 4's *Bake Off: The Professionals*, Benoit is passionate about supporting future pastry chefs.

Having worked in places such as The Ritz hotel in Paris, Benoit has continued to develop throughout his career and has trained with numerous Meilleur Ouvrier de France. In 2005, he was awarded the title of Master of Culinary Arts, MCA, the most prestigious pastry accolade in the UK. In 2009, he was recognised as Pastry Chef of the Year. As its President, Benoit has led the UK pastry team to the Coupe du Monde finals in Lyon, and up until recently, was the Chairman of the UK Pastry Club.

Bake with Benoit Blin is his first book.

Published in 2024 by Hardie Grant Books,
an imprint of Hardie Grant Publishing

Hardie Grant Books (London)
5th & 6th Floors
52—54 Southwark Street
London SE1 1UN

Hardie Grant Books (Melbourne)
Building 1, 658 Church Street
Richmond, Victoria 3121

hardiegrantbooks.com

British Library Cataloguing-in-Publication Data. A catalogue record
for this book is available from the British Library.

Bake with Benoit Blin
ISBN: 978-178488-712-4

10 9 8 7 6 5 4 3 2 1

Publishing Director: Kajal Mistry
Commissioning Editor: Isabel Gonzalez-Prendergast
Copy Editor: Vicky Orchard
Proofreader: Tara O'Sullivan
Design and Art Direction: Nikki Dupin for Studio Nic&Lou
Photographer: Sam Folan
Photographer's Assistant: Gizem Kumbarici
Food Stylist: Lizzie Kamenetzky
Food Stylist's Assistant: Georgia Rudd
Prop Stylist: Jen Kay
Production Controller: Sabeena Atchia

Colour reproduction by p2d
Printed and bound in China by Leo Paper Products Ltd.